The Quality Professor

Implementing TQM in the Classroom

Robert A. Cornesky

Edited by
Jennifer Lind

Editorial assistance from
Robert Magnan
Linda Babler
Peter Vogt
Doris Green

Magna Publications, Inc.

The Quality Professor: Implementing TQM in the Classroom

Printed in the United States of America.

First Edition.

Library of Congress Cataloging-in-Publication Data

Cornesky, Robert A.

The Quality Professor: Implementing TQM in the Classroom / Robert A. Cornesky. -- 1st ed.

   p. cm

Includes bibliographical references.

ISBN 0-912150-29-7

College Teaching
Total quality management
I. Title
LB2331.C65 1991   93-43859
                                              CIP

Cover design by Tamara Cook

Magna Publications, Inc.
2718 Dryden Drive
Madison, WI 53704-3086
608/246-3580

Contents

Introduction

Attempting to teach effectively amid the myriad challenges of the mid-1990s, college and university instructors are running into obstacles and criticisms on all sides. Public cries for adjustments in faculty workload, for reductions in education budgets, and for improvements in student achievement arrive in daily assaults via the media, interdepartmental memos, and campus rallies against higher tuition.

Surrounded by this cacophony, it's sometimes difficult to focus on what's really happening in the classroom and how to improve student learning. Take a moment now to reflect on the relationship of student and instructor. What is their relationship? That is, what roles do they each play in the educational process?

Each student is a "customer." He or she pays for a service — education. You, as the instructor provide the education — or at least the opportunity — as the "vendor."

Each student is a "worker." He or she must put forth effort and perform certain functions in order to learn. You organize, motivate, control, and evaluate the student, functioning as a "manager."

Each student is a "product." He or she is what our system of higher education produces. You are one of many artisans responsible for ensuring the quality of that product.

So the student's relationship to you is that of customer to vendor, worker to manager, and product to artisan, simultaneously. The relationship depends on the specific circumstances, on factors ranging from institutional mission through disciplines and class level to the personalities of the students and you.

There are some basics that define good instruction, however. You should:

1. Assign work that stimulates students to learn, to think critically, and to grow.
2. Guide, motivate, and develop students (workers) without coercion.

v

3. Be aware that coercion begets coercion, and as a result, learning and cooperation decrease.

4. Be aware that empowering the student (worker) increases the number of students who will demonstrate their effectiveness.

Too often, instructors run their classes like traditional managers might. They act like "the boss." They structure and control to the point of stifling, and assume that only the manager — the instructor — knows what's best for all members of the class.

This is as misguided as the belief that only the president knows what's best for the institution. What we have here is an instructor — a person with influence and power — practicing boss-management. He or she expects students to be performing robots, which results in a vicious adversarial cycle: the student learns less and resists more, so the instructor teaches less and coerces more. Not only does this make the job of teaching more difficult, but the cost of education increases, as more instructors are hired and more equipment and supplies are required.

One way to stop this cycle within our colleges and universities is to retrain boss-manager instructors or replace them with lead-manager instructors.

Four essential traits characterize a lead-manager instructor:

1. The instructor must engage the student in a discussion of the quality of the work to be done. He or she listens and incorporates the student's suggestions into the classroom environment.

2. The instructor must demonstrate precisely what is expected of the student — this is the benefit of a course syllabus.

3. The instructor asks the students to inspect their own work, with the assumption that they will care about their efforts and do their very best.

4. Finally, the instructor becomes a facilitator and coach who shows the students that he or she has done everything possible to give them the best tools and workplace as well as a supportive atmosphere in which to do a quality job.

The students' understanding and ownership of the course goals become the road map for everything that happens in the classroom.

In his book on *Achieving Educational Excellence* (Jossey-Bass, 1985), Alexander Astin, director of the Higher Education Research Institute, UCLA, says that students learn while interacting frequently with faculty and other students. Astin says, "If a particular curriculum ... is to have its intended effects, it must elicit enough student effort and investment of energy to bring about the desired learning. Simply exposing the student to a particular set of courses may or may not work."

In general, instructors utilize one of two teaching styles to elicit student effort: "teacher-centered" and "student-centered."

Teacher-centered instructors concentrate on tasks and content. They rarely take time to build networks among students.

Student-centered instructors build relationships and teams. They set goals as they improve teamwork among the students. They dislike performance objectives.

Since each style has its assets and liabilities, the lead-manager instructor integrates each into his or her personal style, while following the hallmarks of good teaching:

- Be well-prepared for class.
- Demonstrate comprehensive subject knowledge.
- Motivate students to take charge of their own learning.
- Be fair.
- Be sincere and interested in the subject matter.

With this in mind, a book on instructor/student communication using a business philosophy may seem like a contradiction in terms. You may be asking, **"Why Total Quality Management?"**

The answer is easy. TQM is a procedure in which everyone strives to continuously improve the path leading to success. TQM is not a rigid set of rules and regulations, but processes and procedures for improving performance.

What you do on your own may be complemented by TQM processes and tools. This text is a map to help you implement TQM in the classroom. It's a way to chart your course and involve everyone in reaching your destination.

So what's happening to our institutions that makes TQM an appropriate alternative? What are the bases of TQM and how do they apply to the classroom? How does TQM treat you, the instructor? How does TQM treat students? How does TQM change the relationship between you and the student? How are results charted?

In the following chapters, we answer these questions and show you how to implement TQM and continuously improve your classroom effectiveness. *The Quality Professor* is structured like a syllabus, beginning with the basic requirements of change, then proceeding to historical background and case studies that demonstrate the use of many TQM tools. A number of the charts and graphs can easily be photocopied and adapted for use in your own classroom. Finally, there is a self-assessment checklist to measure your success.

Chapter One: Focus on Success

"Satisfy the customer, first, last, and always."

Philip Crosby
Let's Talk Quality (1989)

Students walk into your classroom on the first day of class. Each has different goals, expectations, and ambitions in life that in some way relate to your subject. As an instructor, you strive to provide the best education possible for the students, while recognizing their different levels and types of motivation.

But motivation to learn must come from within. It cannot be mandated by you, parents, or others. Everyone has different interests and dreams, and the benefits of your class may not be readily apparent to an unmotivated, "just getting by" student. This may frustrate you.

But the drive to learn is supremely human. People learn in different ways, to varying degrees. The discrepancy comes when some students don't want to learn material in the way you've planned, whether it be lecture, discussion, or experimentation.

TQM offers an answer. While you may know how to best teach your material, you can improve student motivation through teamwork and your suggestions. Students who actively participate in the decision-making process will probably be more successful, develop better critical thinking skills, and become lifelong learners. This is vital if we are going to prepare students to meet the challenges of the next century.

TQM measures the quality of our work. The continuous improvement approach has a long-term, undramatic effect on a process or system. Change is gradual and involves everyone. The resulting group effort focuses on processes and systems rather than on one person's performance evaluation. The approach requires little monetary investment, but a great deal of effort on your part to maintain the group process.

What Are Our Goals?

Philip Crosby states, in *Let's Talk Quality: 96 Questions You Always Wanted to Ask Phil Crosby* (McGraw-Hill, 1989, p. 49):

> If we make our profit goals, but don't pay our bills, then we have not met our profit goals. If we deliver on time, but the product has defects, we have not

11

delivered on time. If we meet our safety objectives, but damage somebody, we have not met our safety objectives.

Crosby's statement applies directly to education. If we say everyone is entitled to a good education, and students drop out because they haven't received that education, we have not met our goal. If we promise to prepare graduates for the future, yet upon graduation they have poor reading skills, poor job skills, or poor preparation for graduate school, they are "defective" and we have not met our goal. If we say we are going to give students a good learning environment, and even one student is harmed by verbal abuse, we have not met our goal.

Have We Reached Our Goals?

We need to improve our processes when students are not reaching their potential. Too many students are leaving college without the skills to become self-sufficient, responsible, concerned citizens and thinkers. Simply put, we're not meeting expectations, and we've got to acknowledge that failure.

I understand your urge as an instructor to rely on word of mouth, or to imagine that no news is good news. The problem with that attitude is that students lose, perhaps by failing or dropping out of school, perhaps by being unable to pursue their career ambitions successfully.

Employers increasingly complain of a diminishing supply of workers who have the skills required for entry-level jobs. Crosby says, "When the corporations of this country tell the schools that they are not satisfied with the way quality and other things are being taught, things will change" (*Let's Talk Quality*, p. 32).

This change is happening now. Mandates from state government threaten to impose major restructuring on the funding process. Mandates represent a level of frustration over the current status of our public colleges and universities that you and other educators can no longer ignore.

In the past, this was not an issue for instructors, simply because there were few options for those who were unhappy with public higher education. Now, many states partially fund private colleges and universities. This represents a potentially major financial loss for some public colleges and universities.

These developments should provide a strong impetus for you to examine any fear you might have of gathering data on the quality of your work. Perhaps your reluctance is outweighed by concerns about who will gather the data, what will be collected, and what will be the outcome. But an active stance on customer satisfaction can help you make alterations within the classroom to improve student achievement and trust.

A Path to Success
TQM allows the customer (your student) to communicate with the decision-maker (you) to continuously improve the educational process.

Generally, the concept of "customers" within educational institutions differs from the general business definition, because in education it's usually undesirable to have "repeat customers." However, if parents, alumni, and students (internal customers) are satisfied with their school experiences, they'll recommend your institution to others. Likewise, if employers and graduate schools (external customers) are satisfied with the graduates of your institution, they'll likely continue their relationship with you.

Thus, parents, students, alumni, employers, and graduate schools share some of the characteristics of traditional customers. The process of improving instruction begins with recognizing **all** of these customers and their expectations.

It's essential to understand that your students aren't merely receptacles to be filled with information. A student is a "customer" paying for a quality education, a "worker" you oversee, and a "product" you shape and develop. This relationship is shown at each level of a college education.

In the first year or in general education courses, your customers include students, parents, and subsequent instructors. Students with deficiencies who move to the next level will be hampered from the beginning. By assessing your classroom practices, you can find ways to improve classroom processes and systems and eliminate deficiencies.

How to Begin TQM
You can begin by systematically collecting data from your customers-students. TQM tools permit you to measure what has occurred within your classroom. In the following chapters, we'll

discuss the Plan-Do-Check-Act cycle, the quality function deployment and house of quality techniques, statistical tools like "control charts," "run charts," and "Pareto Diagrams."

But you can start surveying student expectations and assessing your ability to adapt to those expectations on the first day of class. This first step becomes a continuous process throughout the course.

As with any data collection, a formal, written procedure works best, although collection can be done orally. A word of caution, however: if you choose to collect data orally from students, be aware that your choice of words and responses can skew the data. Also, students, out of fear or in their desire to please you, may be reluctant to respond honestly.

You can also survey other internal customers (colleagues), who can tell you whether they're satisfied with former students. Undergraduate instructors can also use a questionnaire to track their graduates in the careers or graduate school.

The Need for Trust

Instructors demonstrate a lack of trust when they're defensive about having administrators, colleagues, employers, or parents visit the classroom. Without trust, it's doubtful that many instructors will be able to fully develop students to their potential.

Trust dramatically improves the learning climate of the classroom. When you make a sincere effort to listen to **all** students without being judgmental, the students have more reason to trust you. The resulting feedback will provide insights for implementing continuous improvement projects; consequently, students are more likely to take an active role in their education.

Likewise, when instructors, administrators, parents, and public officials listen non-judgmentally to each other, everyone can become partners in the continuous improvement process. Unfortunately, bad publicity has created a wide chasm at a time when these groups need to work together to improve higher education.

Responsible Use of Data

Some of the distrust and bad publicity comes from misuse and incorrect reporting of data. Many instructors may feel that data collection and reporting are out of their hands, and out of their control. It's always easy to blame others, and each of the above groups shares responsibility for this problem. **So remember:**

unless you use data responsibly to resolve problems, there is no valid reason for collecting it.

Data collection takes courage, since it's a signal that you're serious about making changes. In his book *Peak Performance Principles for High Achievers* (Berkley Publishing Group, 1986), John Noe says:

> The great enemy of courage is not cowardice, but conformity. The vast majority of people yield to the pressures of conformity because it is safe. It is unconventional to set your sights high, to climb out of ruts. That takes courage. (p. 110)

It takes courage to use data without blame and shame, with a sense of responsibility for establishing teams to find ways to improve. Be prepared for all of your "customers" to point out areas that need improvement.

But don't be afraid. Often we become overwhelmed by fear of the unknown. As a first step, face the fear that comes from new beginnings. Push through the fear. It's the only way to reap massive, positive results over the long term.

Chapter Two: Total Quality Management Approaches and Principles

"I must close with a warning. Once people have learned to walk, they will not return to crawling. Once students have tasted the joy of learning in an educational institution which runs according to quality management principles, they will not accept something inferior."

Myron Tribus
TQM in Education (1992 pre-publication)

The Deming Approach

Dr. W. Edwards Deming is the father of TQM. His ideas first earned him a following in Japan, where they helped industries rebuild after World War II.

Deming outlined his philosophy by listing 14 points for managing quality and productivity (*Out of the Crisis*, 1986). Although he focused mainly on the manufacturing sector, his points apply to education as well.

His approach is humanistic and treats "workers" as intelligent people who want to do a good job. Deming shows great disdain for managers who hold workers responsible for problems of poor quality. Applying TQM to the classroom, Deming would disagree with instructors who blame the students for not doing a quality job.

The following are Deming's 14 points:

1. Create constancy of purpose for improvement of product and service, with the aim of becoming competitive and staying in business, and to provide jobs.
2. Adopt the new philosophy. We are in a new economic age. Western management must awaken to the challenge, learn its responsibilities, and take on leadership for change.
3. Cease dependence on inspection to achieve quality. Eliminate the need for inspection on a mass basis by building quality into the product in the first place.
4. End the practice of awarding business on the basis of price tag alone. Move toward a single supplier for any one item on the basis of a long-term relationship of loyalty and trust. Minimize total cost by working with a single supplier.
5. Improve constantly and forever every process for planning, production, and service, to improve quality and productivity and thus constantly decrease costs.
6. Institute training on the job.
7. Adopt and institute leadership. The aim of supervision should be to help people and machines and gadgets do a

better job. Supervision of management is in need of an overhaul, as is supervision of production workers.

8. Drive out fear, so that everyone can work effectively for the company.

9. Break down barriers between departments. People in research, design, sales, and production must work as a team to foresee problems of production and those that may be encountered with the product or service.

10. Eliminate slogans, exhortations, and targets for the work force that ask for zero defects or new levels of productivity. Such exhortations only create adversarial relationships, since the bulk of the causes of low quality and productivity belong to the system and thus lie beyond the power of the work force.

11. a. Eliminate work standards (quotas) on the factory floor. Substitute leadership.
b. Eliminate management by objectives. Eliminate management by numbers, and numerical goals. Substitute leadership.

12. a. Remove barriers that rob the hourly worker of his or her right to pride in workmanship. The responsibility of supervisors must be changed from sheer numbers to quality.
b. Remove barriers that rob people in management and engineering of their right to pride in workmanship. This means abolishing the annual or merit rating and management by objective.

13. Institute a vigorous program of education and self-improvement.

14. Put everybody in the company to work to accomplish the transformation. The transformation is everybody's job.

What follows is a brief look at Deming's points and how they might be applied to the classroom.

Point 1: Create a Constancy of Purpose

Many classes have ill-defined and confusing objectives. You and your students should produce an action plan that concentrates on focused objectives, allowing you to meet the present and projected needs of customers of higher education.

Bill Cerbin of the University of Wisconsin-La Crosse uses a course portfolio to create the constancy of purpose (1993, paper delivered at the AAHE Meeting). He states:

> A course portfolio begins with a **Teaching Statement** that conveys the professor's assumptions and beliefs about teaching and learning. It also explains the intended learning outcomes of the course, the teaching practices used to address the learning outcomes, and a rationale that connects the course goals to the professor's methods. A good teaching statement provides a coherent framework for analyzing and evaluating teaching in the class.

(For more information, contact Bill Cerbin, Center for Effective Teaching and Learning, University of Wisconsin-La Crosse, La Crosse, WI 54601.

Point 2: Adopt the New Philosophy

Once you and your students have established the goals and objectives of the class, it is important that you all accept them. This will happen only when you seriously commit to quality and trust.

Point 3: Cease Dependence on Inspection

Quality must be built into our educational processes in order for each student to reach his or her potential. Inspections at the "end of the line" are too late.

At the end of the semester, for example, when students are considering taking the next course in a series, it's too late to go back: we've lost our opportunity to improve student skills. By using TQM, however, you and your students work together to identify problem areas and make necessary changes so that all the students can do quality work.

Inspection is helpful only if it provides information leading to continuous improvement.

Point 4: End the Practice of Awarding Business on the Basis of Price Alone

Stop using the easy methods of teaching and testing.

Point 5: Improve Constantly and Forever

Since it's impossible to achieve "mastery" in every facet of life, people must always strive to improve. This is as true for you as it is for students.

In the classroom, you and your students should constantly seek ways to improve the systems that control achievement levels and enjoyment. When learning is stimulating, everyone will want to contribute.

Point 6: Institute Training on the Job

Quality will not happen unless everyone is adequately trained. You must provide students with information about TQM to derive the greatest benefits from their efforts.

Point 7: Adopt and Institute Leadership

The aim of TQM is to allow students to achieve their potential. By adopting a variety of leadership roles within the classroom, you can empower students to become responsible for their own learning and for the success of their fellow students.

An example of leadership in the classroom can be seen at Xavier University (OH) where Professor Samuel Welch, director of the opera workshop, teaches quality through music.

The music department uses a TQM approach to train opera performers. Through the Opera Workshop, Xavier provides students and faculty with an educational experience that leads to lifelong development of performing skill.

The workshop focuses on teamwork among faculty, administrators, students, and opera industry professionals. It recognizes students as the direct customers of the education process and acknowledges opera company executives — who employ emerging performers — as indirect customers.

The program also emphasizes economic principles and the consequences of meeting or exceeding customer expectations. Continuing research with students, established professional performers, and opera company managers helps determine what's included in the class syllabus.

Students actively study current employment requirements of the opera profession. They also design their programs and evaluate their own and their classmates' improvement in individual and ensemble performances.

What significantly influences the workshop's design is that the students prioritize required professional skills and evaluate those skills by analyzing costs and benefits —— for both the school and the student, if he or she doesn't develop the skills while at Xavier.

(For more information, contact Helmut Roehrig, Chair, or Samuel Welch, Opera Workshop Director, Department of Music, Xavier University, 3800 Victory Parkway, Cincinnati, OH 45207-5511.)

Point 8: Drive Out Fear

You must remove fear from the classroom so that students can work confidently.

When students feel that they're trusted, they'll take pride in their work and quality will improve. As the classroom becomes more stimulating, you and your students will develop collegiality.

Point 9: Break Down Barriers Between Departments

Traditionally, instructors have viewed their classrooms as private domains. In many institutions there is little communication between instructors in different departments.

We must break down these barriers and work together to identify problems and implement changes that will build and maintain quality.

Point 10: Eliminate Slogans and Exhortation

Slogans and exhortations are ineffective in improving quality, unless the instructor shows students how they can achieve quality goals.

Point 11: Eliminate Quotas and Numerical Goals and Substitute Leadership

Deming believes quotas and numerical goals hinder quality more than any single working condition.

Grades based solely on paper-and-pencil tests tend to discourage students from taking active interest in their learning and often encourage them to do the minimum. Traditional grading also promotes isolationism, since competition among students increases.

23

Quotas (grading on the curve) and numerical work standards (performance on standardized exams) discourage collegiality between you and your students.

Point 12: Remove Barriers That Rob
Workers of Their Right to Pride

Trust is vital in the TQM classroom. Without it, students lack encouragement to do quality work.

Classrooms that allow students to set quality goals with meaningful assignments will produce active, enthusiastic, lifelong learners. Students will develop greater pride in their efforts when they work to resolve real problems, especially in teams.

Point 13: Institute a Vigorous Program
of Education and Self-Improvement

The "quality instructor" is aware of the need for personal and professional growth. He or she pursues a plan of continuous self-improvement. This presupposes a professional development plan, with each step leading to greater self-awareness as well as improvement in teaching techniques and strategies.

Harry Roberts of the University of Chicago suggests using a personal checklist to facilitate TQM in your own life.

Point 14: Involve Everyone in the Transformation to Quality

Often, instructors fail to seek, or they ignore, student input on resolving classroom problems. The control issue is a big one for many instructors. As a result, they give orders rather than lead.

In 1987, Red Rocks Community College (CO) began to involve everyone in transforming the curriculum. Campus officials began working with employers to determine what Red Rocks Community College graduates should know upon graduation. Interviewing specialists transcribed all of the information and compiled a list of objectives.

As a result of this work, 11 lists of objectives were produced for each sub-curriculum (program area) — the original list produced in the department and lists produced by each of the 10 employers contacted for that sub-curriculum. After the lists were generated, the specialists deleted duplicate terms and created a final list of measurable objectives.

Finally, the lists went back to the department chairs, who reviewed them. The lists were usually reviewed further in department meetings. If changes were made, the group of 10 employers had another chance to respond.

The next step in the sub-curriculum work was delivery of the "final" sub-curriculum objective list to the respective department chairs, with instructions for designating the specific courses required for a certificate or degree program that best fit each objective.

(For more information, contact Joe Franklin, Manager, Automated Instructional Management System, Red Rock Community College, 13300 W. Sixth Ave., Box 34, Lakewood, CO 80401-5398.)

The Deming philosophy establishes an atmosphere that supports ongoing improvement. Quality must be part of the classroom culture. Without it, students cannot take pride in their work.

Deming believes quality is never a problem, but a solution to a problem. He supports the concept that the organized activity of work takes place in a system where at least 85% of the systems are controlled by management (instructors) and 15% or less are controlled by workers (students).

Your main job is to improve the systems, with the help of your students, so that a higher level of quality can be achieved.

Deming believes a quality manager responds to the problems of *systems* and the problems of *people* simultaneously.

The Crosby Approach

The philosophy of Philip Crosby (*Quality Without Tears: The Art of Hassle-Free Management,* McGraw-Hill, 1984) enforces the belief that quality is a universal goal, and that management must provide the leadership to ensure that an enterprise *never* compromises quality.

Crosby believes that the system of quality is based on prevention. He encourages a performance standard of zero defects and says that the measurement of quality is the price of non-conformance — doing something over rather than doing it right the first time. He believes managers should be *facilitators* and should be considered as such by employees.

Like Deming, Crosby (1984, p. 99) has 14 steps for quality improvement:

25

1. Commitment from management
2. Quality improvement team
3. Measurement
4. Cost of quality
5. Quality awareness
6. Corrective action
7. Zero defects planning
8. Employee education
9. Zero defects day
10. Goal-setting
11. Error-cause removal
12. Recognition
13. Quality councils
14. Do it over again

We again consider how these points might apply to the classroom.

Point 1: Instructor's Commitment
Before lasting change toward quality can be realized, you must be trained in quality processes and systems, and it must be clear that you're going to support the commitment to quality.

Point 2: Quality Improvement Team
In order to involve the entire class in adopting the new quality philosophy, you should form a team consisting of students representing factions of the student body. As problems are identified, you should form additional teams to work on an action plan for resolution.

For example, in fall 1990, Ian Hau was teaching a large undergraduate statistics course at the University of Wisconsin-Madison. From the students in his class, Hau formed a small team to help him improve the course while he was teaching it.

(For more information, order Report No. 59, *Teaching Quality Improvement by Quality Improvement in Teaching*, by Ian Hau, February 1991, Center for Quality and Productivity Improvement, University of Wisconsin, 610 Walnut St., Madison, WI 53706.)

Point 3: Measurement

You should gather baseline data to evaluate the improvement process. You and your students won't know how you're doing if such data are not available; consequently you all become frustrated. If you and your students are uncertain about how you're progressing toward announced quality goals, you'll become frustrated and operate under your own rules.

Point 4: The Cost of Quality

You should conduct special training on record-keeping for all students so that they can establish a procedure for evaluation. The evaluation procedure should be consistent throughout the process.

At the University of Chicago, for example, professors George Bateman and Harry Roberts draw instructors and students closer together through feedback (from students) and "reverse feedback" (from instructors). In their opinion:

> Written reverse feedback from instructor to student can literally open a second channel of communication. For example, the instructor can provide explanations of points singled out by the fast-feedback questionnaires, and even answer specific questions asked on the questionnaires by students.
> Reverse feedback can mean substantial time and effort by the instructor, but the payback in avoidance of rework is large for students and instructors alike.

(For more information, contact George Bateman or Harry Roberts, Graduate School of Business, University of Chicago, 1101 E. 58th St., Chicago, IL 60637.)

Point 5: Quality Awareness

Quality must become part of your class culture. Students, employers, and administrators should understand that you are committed to quality, that *quality is the policy*. You must teach the students the cost doing a task incorrectly.

Point 6: Corrective Action

The main purpose of corrective action is to identify problems and take actions necessary to eliminate their root causes.

Corrective action focuses on eliminating system and process mistakes. Students are empowered to alert you to things that could be done more efficiently within a no-blame atmosphere. This requires teamwork between you and students and among groups of students.

Bateman and Roberts report that instructors acted immediately to their questionnaires:

- One instructor installed a portable microphone after students said they were having trouble hearing him.
- Another instructor left the lights on and used larger type after students said they were having trouble seeing the overhead.
- A third instructor moved to other material more rapidly in class after students said they didn't need to cover material read in advance.
- A fourth instructor used more examples in class, following student suggestions.

Point 7: Zero Defects Planning

Whereas corrective action is hindsight, zero defects planning is foresight. It comes from identifying possible problems and implementing a way to prevent them.

Everyone benefits from zero defects planning, because it presupposes that no one will leave the classroom with less than "mastery."

Point 8: Employee Education

After you learn about TQM, you must train your students in the philosophy and procedures. This may take several hours or the equivalent of several class periods. Students might even have an entire course on continuous improvement, possibly as part of the first-year experience.

Point 9: Zero Defects Day

Crosby believes a celebration is important when the group is trained and ready to launch its zero defects philosophy. In the classroom this might mean a special celebration when your students are educated in TQM.

Point 10: Setting Goals

Setting goals is crucial to the success of every student and every instructor. Goals provide a road map to achievement. By making goal-setting a regular, integral part of your day, you and your students will have a clear focus that will direct all behavior toward quality.

Point 11: Error-Cause Removal

When you recognize errors, it's important to institute a program to eliminate them quickly, using TQM tools. As an educator, you can help students realize where process mistakes are made and provide corrective action.

Point 12: Recognition

Crosby believes in providing recognition for achievement. He recognizes that team efforts are more important than individual efforts. Teamwork is one of the cornerstones of TQM: it empowers students to resolve problems and work for the success of the organization.

Professor Peter Haugh of Western Washington University wrote the following about how he recognizes his Student Advisory Committee (SAC):

> At the end of the course, I use several techniques to reinforce the importance of the SAC. During one of the last classes, I present Distinguished Service Awards to each SAC participant, and then I take the members to lunch. These events highlight the importance of the SACs and are passed on by word of mouth to future students.

(For more information contact Peter Haugh, Management Department, Western Washington University, 516 High St., Bellingham, WA 98225.)

Point 13: Quality Councils

Crosby (1984) states that "the idea of quality councils is to bring the quality professionals together and let them learn from each other" (p. 119). This is an excellent way to keep the organization focused on "quality" issues and to prevent slipping back into traditional manners of operation.

Whereas Deming encourages total involvement between the customer and the supplier, Crosby's point on instituting "quality councils" ensures that everyone in your classroom will stay focused.

Point 14: Do It Over Again

Since the quality journey is continuous, you and your students should continuously apply what you've learned to improve your teaching/learning system.

Principles of Total Quality Management

In the previous section, we identified the TQM models of Deming and Crosby. Although different in some respects, they have common elements.

The purpose of this section is to examine the common elements of these quality experts and suggest how those elements might be applied in the classroom.

The seven common elements that bind the foundations of TQM by Deming and Crosby are:

- Processes and Systems,
- Teaming,
- Customers and Suppliers,
- Quality by Fact, Process, and Perception,
- Management by Fact,
- Complexity,
- Variation.

Let's examine each of these common elements.

Processes and Systems

All of the combined tasks or steps necessary to accomplish a given result are defined as a *process*.

Every work activity is part of a process and system. It follows that classroom learning can improve only if the processes and systems improve. If you as the instructor improve the processes and systems, your students will perform better and become more productive.

A *system*, as used in this text, means an arrangement of persons, places, things, and/or circumstances that makes, facilitates, or permits things to happen.

Examples of classroom systems include teaching methods, grading procedures, and assignments. The very nature of a system will determine what will happen and how.

In the classroom, most instructors face the challenge of maintaining the strengths and eliminating the weaknesses of systems established by their predecessors. Most likely, they have entered situations where anticipated results yield predictable attitudes and behaviors.

This cycle of predictability can change toward quality, as illustrated in Figure 2.1.

Figure 2.1: Process inhibiting change to quality

Results

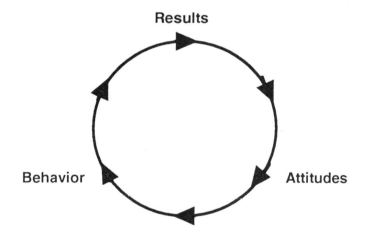

Behavior   **Attitudes**

If you control 85%-90% of the classroom processes and systems, you can influence students to seriously commit to quality. Every student is different, but all have the capacity to achieve quality work in a supportive atmosphere.

Quality is "contagious." Quality results can lead to improved attitudes, modified behaviors, and a classroom culture focusing on quality. An example of this process is shown in Figure 2.2.

Figure 2.2: Process and results of introducing change to quality

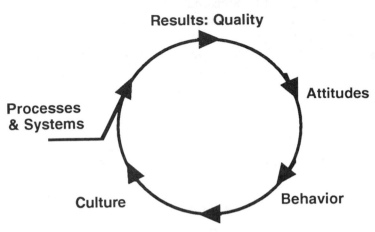

Teaming

Teams and teamwork are extremely important in producing a quality service or product. Although hierarchy is needed within all organizations to avoid chaos, most classroom learning can be accomplished across, not within, organizational boundaries.

The informal power structure and the resulting classroom culture do not readily permit collegiality in a management system based on hierarchy. But with proper teaming (cooperative learning), quality work can result.

Robert Waterman, in his book *Adhocracy: The Power to Change* (1990), refers to a means for motivating active involvement in embracing and effecting change. Waterman suggests that people, under the proper leadership, will participate in meaningful activities with the intention of improving the quality of their organization. This philosophy can be found in the classroom whenever students are engaged with the instructor and with other students.

At Samford University (AL), Kathy Baugher had enormous success teaching student teams to work with instructors to continuously improve teaching and learning. Students from quality teams help instructors make changes in their courses that will enable more students to comprehend the material being covered.

Baugher's *LEARN* manual guides student team members to:
- **L**ocate an opportunity for improvement,
- **E**stablish a team,
- **A**ssess the current process,
- **R**esearch causes, and
- **N**ominate a solution.

In contrast to traditional course evaluations — the kind that are given at the end of a class and furnish generic information for use in future classes — student teams provide continuous evaluation throughout the class that can assist the instructor in improving learning opportunities for current students.

(For more information, contact Kathryn H. Baugher, Dean of Admissions, Belmont University, 1900 Belmont Blvd., Nashville, TN 37212.)

Customers and Suppliers

Satisfied students, parents, alumni, and employers share some of the characteristics of traditional customers by recommending an institution to others or hiring more students from an institution.

Another parallel to the customer concept lies in the instructor-student relationship. The student is a worker and product that you oversee and develop. The student is also a customer paying for knowledge and development. You use processes and systems to supply services to students, employers, and society. You and your students are empowered when you constantly improve the student-worker and instructor-manager relationship.

With empowerment comes trust. With trust comes pride in workmanship. And with pride in workmanship comes teamwork.

If you want to learn more about developing leadership skills, Charles C. Manz and Henry P. Sims, Jr. have published an excellent guide, *Super-Leadership* (Berkley Publishing Group, 1990).

Quality by Fact, Process, and Perception

The quality instructor examines quality from at least three different perspectives:
- Does the education meet the specified goals?
- Does the teaching process and/or system work as intended?
- Does the instruction meet the expectations of the students, the parents, and the employers?

It's conceivable that a course can have quality by fact and by process, yet the customers — either the students or the employers — may not perceive that quality. Education is a lifelong process, where critical thinking skills reap benefits over the long run. TQM's goal is to ensure that you and your students work together to create the best possible system of learning, rather than assume the current one is the only way.

Management by Fact

All leaders in the study of quality emphasize the need for complete and comprehensive data prior to making major decisions.

One simple rule must apply in determining the mission of your course or even in setting out to improve a simple process: your research data should be complete, accurate, and freely available to everyone.

The free availability of information serves two purposes. First, when people know the facts, they can offer essential advice. Second, they can call attention to a serious flaw in a developing plan.

Whenever possible, you should base your decisions on data rather than hunches or assumptions. Data and facts uncover the root of the problem, not just the symptoms, so that you can develop permanent solutions rather than quick fixes.

Complexity

Quality leaders realize the complexity of most processes and systems that create a product or service.

In the classroom, complexity can be defined as extra steps added to a process to recover from errors in the preceding educational experience of your students.

Variation

Every process involving humans and/or machines displays variation. In education, we see wide variation and diversity in students, in the teaching/learning process, and graduates. Excessive variation, however, causes the processes and systems to be erratic and unpredictable. Mediocrity and poor quality result.

Since every process shows variation, no two products — components, services, reports, teaching effectiveness, or graduates — will ever be identical. Your goal, therefore, should be to increase the uniformity and quality of classroom processes.

On Your Way

Although we have borrowed from quality leaders many of the principles advocated here, you may wish to use the following key points to develop your own TQM philosophy:

- Educate yourself and commit to TQM.
- Educate your students and motivate them to commit to TQM.
- Establish trust.
- Establish pride in workmanship.
- Change the classroom culture.

Educate Yourself and Commit to TQM

Since TQM is a deviation from typical supervisory techniques, you should undergo training on its principles. Once you understand TQM, you commit yourself to following its principles. To achieve lasting change, you must make it clear that you are going to support the commitment to quality.

Educate Your Students and Motivate Them to Commit to TQM

Educating your students is critical to the success of TQM. Students should understand quality philosophies and processes and be trained in the tools and techniques they'll use.

The obvious reason for educating students in TQM is that their participation is essential for the processes to work. Most students will make a commitment after they realize that you respect and value their contributions toward improving quality.

Establish Trust

One of the main functions of TQM is to show constant improvement in the quality of education through measurement.

Initially, however, students may consider the process of gathering data and identifying problems as a threat. The only way to overcome this misperception is to establish trust, since people cannot flourish if intimidated.

The first step in establishing trust is to explain the need for comprehensive measurements. Your explanations should show how data can:

35

- demonstrate trends in student satisfaction levels, including satisfaction with you and other students,
- determine whether you are fulfilling your mission and achieving quality goals,
- show the governing board that your institution is becoming more efficient and productive, and
- let the students know how well they and their classmates are performing.

The second step is to inform your students that most of the measurements will be made by them and will be relevant to their needs. They should also know that the measurements will be simple, understandable, and few.

The third step is for you to get involved in measuring your own effectiveness and making honest judgments from the data.

As students become more involved in changing the processes and systems, you must focus your attention on trust and empowerment. We'll discuss this idea further in Chapter 4, Human Resource Development and Management.

Establish Pride in Workmanship

One outcome of dedicated efforts toward improving for quality is that empowered students begin to improve classroom processes and systems. When they're rewarded and recognized for their efforts, they have greater learning satisfaction, improved morale, and improved productivity.

Change the Classroom Culture

The basic philosophy of every quality leader is based upon principles of managing the institutional culture, not the people. "Managing" does not necessarily mean "controlling." If control is your main goal, it will be difficult for you to achieve quality.

Students won't relinquish their rights to individuality to a cookie-cutter approach. It's up to you to balance individualization and team cooperation.

Leadership, according to John W. Gardner (*On Leadership*, The Free Press, 1990, p.1), is the *process of persuasion or example* by which an individual (or leadership team) *induces a group to pursue objectives* held by the leader or shared by the leader and followers.

Gardner says leadership must not be confused with status, power, or official authority. Leaders are affected by the system in which they work. Leaders perform tasks that allow others to improve the quality of services and/or products.

As quality improves in your classroom, so will the students' pride in workmanship. The end result will be a new classroom culture in which students are motivated to grow and develop.

A Cycle of Action

Once you and your students feel comfortable with implementing TQM, you can chart a plan of action with the Deming Plan-Do-Check-Act (P-D-C-A) cycle (Figure 2.3).

Figure 2.3: Example of the Deming Plan-Do-Check-Act Cycle

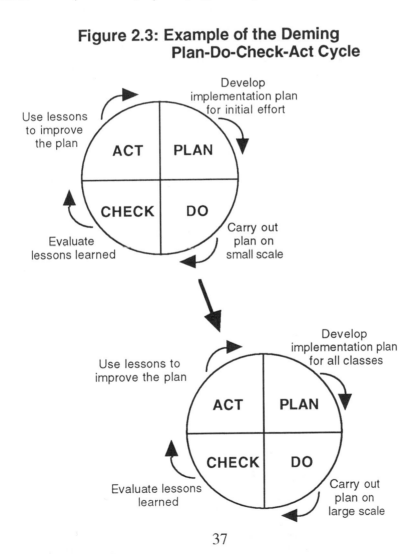

The first step, *plan,* requires you to carefully review the goals of your class. With these goals as a focal point, you can form a quality team to uncover problems (based on data) and seek possible solutions.

It's important to establish a consensus on the best plan; otherwise, you run the risk of having less than total commitment from your students.

The TQM tools necessary to accomplish this objective (presented in Chapters 7 and 8) include the Nominal Group Process, the Affinity Diagram, the Cause-and-Effect Diagram, the Force Field Analysis, the Pareto Diagram, the House of Quality technique, the Run Chart, the Systematic Diagram, the Scenario Builder, the Histogram, Flow Charts, and Control Charts.

The next step in your action plan is *do.* Simply stated, this means that everyone must be dedicated to carrying out the plan. A flow chart is drawn showing where changes will be made. You should post it alongside a flow chart of the original classroom system to show changes in the process.

Once you've followed through on the plan long enough to allow it to work, there is an assessment, or *check* phase. At this point, you study whether or not the implemented changes have produced the desired results. Remember, "checking" does not simply mean evaluation by you. It includes empowering your students to assess their work and the work of their classmates.

Finally, *act* by using the evaluative data to improve the process. Make changes when the data provide evidence of problems.

Chapter Three: Leadership

*"Our chief want in life is somebody
who will make us do what we can."*

Ralph Waldo Emerson

Take time to briefly answer the following questions before reading this chapter and answering the questions on the subsequent checksheet, so that you can examine your commitment as a leader of students who helps them achieve quality work.

Describe what quality means to you. If you have a formal statement, please write it out.

How have you shared the quality policy and/or mission statement of your class with your students?

Describe your leadership, personal involvement, and visibility in communicating the quality program to your colleagues, outside employers, the community, administration, and other groups.

Describe your preferred teaching style.

Describe the nature of any ongoing education that you have taken to keep up with the latest trends in your discipline.

How do you define quality in your work? Explain the ways you exemplify that to your colleagues.

Leadership is probably the most important ingredient in establishing quality in any organization, including the classroom. As Deming says in his seventh and 11th points:

7. Adopt and institute *leadership*. The aim of supervision should be to help people, machines, and gadgets do a better job. Supervision of management is in need of an overhaul, as is supervision of production workers.

11a. Eliminate work standards (quotas) on the factory floor. Substitute *leadership*.

11b.   Eliminate management by objectives. Eliminate management by numbers and numerical goals. Substitute *leadership.*

Applied to the classroom, Deming's seventh point might read:
Adopt and institute *leadership.* Your aim should be to help students do a better job.

His 11th point might read:
Eliminate the traditional, standardized grading system from the classroom. Eliminate management by objectives and numbers. Substitute *leadership,* making sure that what the students learn, they learn well.

The Quality Instructor as Super-Leader

One of Deming's key observations is that 85% of the systems in which people work are controlled by managers, while only 15% are controlled by workers. This statement speaks loudly to institutions of higher education, and only recently have many begun looking seriously at management as a meaningful place to begin restructuring efforts.

In classrooms, the systems are those things that determine the climate, or "feel," of the learning environments, such as:
• teaching style,
• organization of materials,
• assignments, and
• evaluation methods.

Changes in any of these systems can result in changes in student attitudes, behavior, and work quality.

The Roles of the Super-Leader

To achieve change in the classroom, you'll have to assume a new role for the 21st century. Your goal will be not only to have students achieving at the 85% level or higher, but also to have students always looking for ways to improve their world, their beliefs, and their society.

Students who have been taught in this manner will survive and thrive in our complex, ever-changing technological society. Our students will not be frightened by change because they will have been taught to accept change as a way of life.

A quality instructor reaches not only the academically gifted student, but also the student who may need more time to learn a fact or concept. A quality instructor establishes a classroom climate conducive to universal success because he or she believes in the worth of *all students.* He or she encourages students to stretch their intellectual limits to achieve superior knowledge and problem-solving abilities. He or she is a *"super-leader"* who instills in students a sense of inquisitiveness and desire for learning.

Such an ideal, however, requires you to take a very different role within the classroom — one that will require more preparation, flexibility, and questioning. Governing boards, employers, and administrators must also be educated about the changing roles of instructors. They must encourage instructors to become super-leaders, who will expect excellence of themselves as well as of their students.

Self-Defined by Improvement

This changing self-definition stems from the ongoing dialogue, questioning, researching, and evaluating that cannot be accomplished in a one-directional style. Critical thinking skills demand that you guide students through a process that ultimately ends with empowerment and expanded knowledge for all of you.

The TQM model is predicated on continuous improvement — that is, change for you and your students. The TQM approach gives the class an opportunity to become a team to resolve problems. It thus becomes everyone's responsibility to resolve problems; no longer is it just your obligation.

None of this improvement comes, however, unless you take time to educate your students.

Constantly Improving Role Model

One way for you to educate and empower students is by being a role model. That involves attention and motivation. Be a model of self-discipline. Be interested in learning. Respect others and their opinions You'll see students stretching their abilities and interests continuously to become self-leaders.

Empowering students means showing respect. It means leading students and allowing them to work together or individually,

43

knowing that if they are given the proper tools to do the job, they'll want to do it well.

A quality instructor understands the need for students to have pride in their work and will not deprive the students of that opportunity. Simply put, you understand that unempowered students will be less inclined to achieve high personal goals or want to contribute to the goals of the class.

Quality instructors see themselves as guides for students. They not only provide the materials with which to achieve the necessary goals, but also act as resource persons, researching the subject matter and being available to the students. Quality instructors don't see themselves as *experts* who know all the answers, but rather as *helpers* who have a solid understanding of the subject matter.

Quality instructors recognize that there are many ways of looking at problems. They remain open and responsive to students. For them, actions speak much louder than words, and as they implement TQM, they are very cognizant of their modeling role. They are eager to provide assistance, learn more, and learn from the students, thus becoming the students' coach and cheerleader.

In the "coaching" role, the quality instructor uses goal-setting, self-evaluation, self-reinforcement, self-motivation, and critical thinking to help students learn complex concepts. He or she assumes responsibility for adequately teaching TQM principles and statistical tools, to empower all students to begin the work of continuous improvement. As a cheerleader, the quality instructor provides encouragement and rewards for the students' journey toward quality work.

The quality instructor encourages team play and interaction with other students. Students work collaboratively, solving problems of increasing difficulty in using teamwork. Students develop the ability to work in teams for the benefit of others, using the principles of justice and fair play. They also respect others, realizing that the success of the class depends on the success of each individual.

Students Become Role Models

Students also assume a primary role in evaluating each other's work. All students are trained in evaluative techniques as well as identification of quality work. A wonderful by-product is that these students regain a "real" place within the classroom. And as their self-esteem grows, their rate of academic achievement increases dramatically.

Indeed, in classrooms across the nation where this is currently happening, even students with minimal skills demonstrate improved self-esteem as each becomes a "helper" to fellow students. Again, you recognize the importance of teaching students to critique others' work without negative messages, but with a systematic method for stretching the skills of each other.

Negative Side Effects?

Expect students to test your sincerity about empowering them to become more responsible for their own learning. Once students recognize that you're sincere and committed to this style, their self-confidence will soar. You will find the need to reinforce the *will* to continuous education and the willingness to share this knowledge with the students. Dare to be different. Don't let setbacks spoil your new instructional style.

Some instructors feel that setbacks include students who are uninterested in learning, unmotivated, and unwilling to do the work. These instructors have chosen to lower standards to accommodate what they perceive as a general lethargy on the part of the students. Along with this comes the notion that K-12 teachers are responsible for not providing the students with a good education that prepares them for college work.

Blaming students and K-12 teachers for the current crisis in higher education has not improved the system or the results. We must understand that reasons for the problem are complex, involving home, society, and school. Blaming people will not resolve the problem, and in fact may exacerbate it.

Adopting the new TQM philosophy requires major attitudinal changes on the part of all educators, including those who make administrative decisions. If we take seriously the notion that everyone wants to develop his or her potential, then we simply have to look at our own philosophy and how it drives what is done within the classroom. This means that we must commit to maintaining a success orientation so that *the new success philosophy includes all students.*

Lifelong Enthusiasm

The quality instructor maintains a leadership role on campus by assisting colleagues. He or she actively participates in professional activities, continuously striving to improve in subject knowledge as well as current teaching practices. The end result is a greater knowledge base, a sense of community, pride in work, and energy to work toward constant improvement.

One way for you to collaborate with other instructors is to coordinate assignments with colleagues from other disciplines. In essence, you can create a learning community within your institution. Learning communities allow students to enjoy the expertise of more than one instructor and consolidate many assignments into one. The result is a much greater depth of knowledge and expertise on the part of each student, which translates into pride in work.

The quality instructor also recognizes the need for maintaining a personal continuous improvement approach to life. Establishing a regular pattern of goal-setting in your personal and professional lives makes you a good role model for students.

Professionally, this means establishing development plans and vigorously pursuing them through conferences, workshops, courses, and professional journals.

Personally, this means recognizing the importance of achieving balance between your professional life and your personal life. Goal-setting and planning are important factors in maintaining a high level of satisfaction and stress management. You may decide, for example, that you don't get enough exercise or that you should pursue a hobby. Learning something new through a hobby or class may provide you with another way to excite students about learning — and maintain your own interest.

Your desire and enthusiasm for knowledge and adventure will be a source of renewal each day, whereas focusing all your energy on students and teaching will eventually wear you out. *All* students (especially at-risk students) need instructors who respect and care for themselves by maintaining a balance in their lives. Your students need a good role model who demonstrates this balance. You can be that role model.

The following is a checksheet tool that can help you baseline your leadership skills. There are six subcategories. Circle the point next to the criterion that most nearly describes your present classroom situation.

Describe what quality means to you. If you have a formal statement, please write it out.

Points   Criteria

1   I have no formal statement.

2   I only mention quality work at the beginning of the class, with no formal statements or examples.

3   I give a formal statement to students and share it with employers, business and community leaders, and administrators.

4   I present a formal statement to my students at the beginning of the class; I display quality work for all to use as a model. Students know what quality work means to their own success and to the success of the class and institution.

5   My formal statement relates to students and the expectations of other customers. I'm committed to continuous improvement in the processes and systems of the classroom and student outcomes.

How have you deployed the quality policy and/or mission statement of your class among the students?

Points   Criteria

1   We mainly "talk" about quality.

2   There is a quality manual on display in the classroom with examples of quality work enclosed.

3   I distribute a quality manual and/or policy statements about quality to all the students.

4   I train all students on quality procedures and goals.

5   I share the quality policy with a clear direction. My students and I work together to improve the classroom activities.

Describe your leadership, personal involvement, and visibility in communicating the quality program to your colleagues, employers, the community, administration, and other groups.

Points   Criteria

1   I use a traditional management role of directing and controlling.

2   My leadership concerning quality issues is visible at my institution.

3   My leadership is visible in expressing our quality mission to governing boards, industry, city officials, and state officials.

4   I'm active in supporting adhocracy and collaborative learning in the classroom. I implement suggestions resulting from student input. I'm a supportive leader for *all* students because I monitor progress and constantly seek ways to improve the learning process.

5   I'm recognized outside the institution as a leader for quality .

Describe your preferred teaching styles.

Points   Criteria

1   I generally lecture, with some question-and-answer periods.

2   I use lecture, demonstration, and question-and-answer periods.

3   I use more traditional methods, along with group work and research assignments.

4   I use a variety of methods, adapting to the learning styles of students and including some collaborative learning.

5   My classes are mostly student-led, stressing collaborative learning and goal-setting. Students master basic facts in a variety of ways. Students with different learning styles work together, which gives them opportunities to contribute in a variety of ways.

Describe the nature of any ongoing education/training you've taken to keep up with the latest trends in your content area.

Points   Criteria

1   I meet the institutional requirements for annual increments each year.

2   I subscribe to at least one professional journal and attend at least one workshop or conference each year.

3   I maintain communication with local and state curriculum specialists, read and implement the latest information, and attend as many conferences as possible.

4   I make recommendations to the librarian for purchases and send for information on the latest trends in my discipline. I encourage specialists to visit my classroom to provide demonstrations and/or offer suggestions for improvements. I read journals and newspapers to implement the newest trends, and I make meaningful assignments in concert with world events.

5   I actively participate in national, state, and local organizations, and cultivate a network with other professionals. I maintain an ongoing, well-planned continuing education program that revolves around a long-term, global perspective.

How do you define quality in your own work? Explain the ways you exemplify that to your colleagues.

Points	Criteria
1	I have given no thought to quality.
2	I define quality by the traditional evaluation by management.
3	I define quality by the achievements of the students, and I present this data in written form to my colleagues.
4	The quality of my work is reflected in the students' enthusiasm for learning and achieving. As a super-leader, I'm available to assist my colleagues.
5	The quality of my work is reflected in the "world-class" quality of students' work and their enthusiasm for helping their classmates succeed. The number of students who pursue a career in my discipline or enroll in advanced courses in my discipline also provides a measure of the quality of my work. Finally, my students and I are having fun learning.

Chapter Four: Human Resource Development and Management

"Everyone might well ask himself every day what he has done this day to advance his learning and skill on this job, and how he has advanced his education for greater satisfaction in life."

W. Edwards Deming
Out of the Crisis (1986)

Take time to briefly answer the following questions before reading this chapter and answering the questions on the subsequent checksheet. Doing so will help you examine the outcomes of your efforts to develop and use the full potential of all your students to maintain an environment conducive to full participation and continuous improvement.

What are your key strategies for increasing the effectiveness, productivity, and participation of *all* students?

Please describe how you educate students in quality improvement.

What percentage of your current students have received education in quality improvement concepts and processes?

Describe how you positively reinforce students for contributions to quality improvement (*e.g.*, recognition of teams, awards).

What have you done to ensure the quality of life in your classroom, maintain a supportive educational environment, and empower students to actively participate in the learning process? If you have examples, please include them.

Constant Communication

Using TQM means that communication is both vertical and horizontal. Traditional classrooms use vertical communication, essentially excluding students from the decision-making process. TQM encourages horizontal communication, which is crucial to the success of the TQM model. As an instructor, you'll need to establish new ways of thinking about horizontal communication and how you can use it to ensure continuous improvement.

If we don't spend enough time explaining to students *why* our subject matter concerns them, then they're more likely to be disinterested — especially if there is no clearly defined connection between the subject matter and their lives. Before you can communicate effectively with your students, however, you must understand the goals of the class. This reiterates Deming's second point: eliminate management by objectives by *establishing a constancy of purpose.*

Establishing a constancy of purpose requires that you talk to your colleagues and external customers. You must understand your institution's mission and how your classroom mission ties into it.

You can't take the search for a classroom mission lightly. The search will probably send you on a journey to self-assessment and evaluation of your own principles regarding the teaching/learning process. It presupposes that you will take time to research the latest ideas of educators, both within and outside your area of specialization, and put these together with your own philosophy of education.

It's important to take this journey thoughtfully, as it will be the guiding force of your work. Avoid the temptation to rush the process or believe that your mission is "a given" (*e.g.,* to teach general chemistry to first-year students and organic chemistry to majors). With careful thought and research, you can establish some insights that you otherwise may not have. Those insights will provide clear guidelines and direction for all the activities in which your students engage.

Define your classroom mission and how all students fit into that mission. Maintain a clear focus on the mission. Be specific. Answer the question: "What do you want your students to accomplish and how?"

The mission statement should be concise and easy to understand. Write it down, give it to your students, and post it prominently in the classroom. Everyone, including your students, must understand the mission so that all can work to achieve it.

Your mission statement can be printed in each student's *House of Quality* book. (See the Quality Function Deployment Tool in Chapter 8.) This will help everyone maintain a clear focus. The *House of Quality* book also becomes vital for teaching TQM principles and setting goals and classroom rules.

Training in TQM principles is necessary for achieving a true quality classroom. You must give students the basic tools of TQM to help them continuously improve.

Education is best accomplished by selecting a project team and a project that requires "fixing" processes and systems. That way you can effectively measure an increase in quality. The chair of your cross-functional team should not be the perceived "expert," nor you (Waterman, *Adhocracy*, 1990, p. 23). The team should consist of 10 or fewer people and should represent as many social units as there are in the class.

After the project team is formed, it must have:

- consistent support from you,
- baseline data to demonstrate improvements,
- time for regular meetings,
- recognition of team success and positive efforts.

Eventually, you should implement the students' suggestions as much as possible. Measure the results of the new process and/or system and reward the team if improvement occurs. Don't punish the team if there is no improvement. After all, it's far better to have tried and failed than not to have tried at all.

Remove Barriers to Success

Who can take pride in mediocrity? Depression is more likely in institutions where expectations for both students and instructors are low.

When your students feel that no one cares about their work, pride disappears and work becomes drudgery for them and for you. No one is happy, because no one seems to care.

On the other hand, the quality instructor will provide challenges for students that require them to stretch their limits.

Students who've never been expected to do quality work will have no idea what it is. They'll be unable to do quality work unless you:

- believe they can do it,
- are available to coach and assist them, and
- provide feedback and the opportunity to improve.

The concept of quality work is one with which even you as an instructor may be unfamiliar. This should not be too surprising, especially if institutional standards aren't very high.

The quest for quality begins with providing examples of quality work from previous classes or other students. This is part of *mastery learning,* as opposed to *mystery learning.*

It's a mistake to believe that quality is easy to understand and promote. Therefore, you must seek examples of true quality work for your students to model. If no examples exist from your previous class or even within your college, find information from campuses identified as excellent. (A list of colleges and universities currently involved in the TQM movement appeared in the October 1993 issue of *Quality Progress*, published by the American Society for Quality Control in Milwaukee.)

Instilling pride in work also involves having the proper tools and equipment to prepare students to perform the task. However, avoid the temptation to blame lack of resources for low student achievement. There are many examples of campuses where students lack resources but do outstanding work.

Preparation for assignments is essential. Preparation means you lay the groundwork and introduce students to the topic or problem. This does not imply that you will give the answers to the class. On the contrary, introduction should encourage students to ask questions about the assignment. The students will want to discover how to do the assignment, whether it's a cooperative learning activity or an individual problem.

If you're a math instructor, for example, you might begin your calculus class by having students get into groups to solve a puzzling question of higher-order mathematics. You could teach the group to become model investigators, looking for clues to solve the puzzle. You could give each person time to ponder the question first and jot down his or her thinking. Then, the group could discuss it and build a consensus.

Class discussion would be lively, as each group would proceed with its logic and conclusions. You would use this as a demonstration for engaging students in the logic of higher mathematics and point out the possibility for more than one method to determine the answer. By the end of the period, you could eliminate many of the students' fears about how difficult your course will be and expand their views of mathematics.

Indeed, this is one way mathematics education is being revolutionized. Many educators now advocate having students work in groups on all problems.

Imagine presenting a real-life math problem to the students, then asking them to form groups to discover the answer. Each group keeps notes on the steps it follows so that when the class comes together to discuss the answer, each group can check its logic for accuracy. As students recognize flaws in their logic, they learn about themselves. No one feels bad and everyone understands the concepts presented by that particular math problem.

The expectations are clearly spelled out for all students, and each understands his or her role. In the TQM classroom, rules and course competencies result from a consensus among you, your students, and other customers (employers, graduate schools) at the beginning of each semester. The purpose is to provide easily understandable parameters in which the students know they can operate.

There is no penalty for making or correcting mistakes. In fact, you should tell students to view mistakes as a natural path to growth — an opportunity to gain greater insight as they spawn continuous improvement projects. The classroom atmosphere is one of genuine friendliness, cooperation, and eagerness to help others reach maximum potential. You should encourage questioning and critical thinking. Students should find answers together, with you actively engaging in the process.

Capitalize on students' natural desire to help others by encouraging them to participate in the most rigorous endeavors possible. Emphasize learning styles and provide the tools necessary for students to do a good job. Expect students to help their classmates reach the goals of the class. Help them work with partners or in small groups to assist their classmates.

Students need to do meaningful work. Meaningful class assignments can greatly increase students' motivation to do quality work.

One way to increase students' motivation is to relate your assignments to the "real world." For example:

> If you're an English composition instructor, you might relate the class to the growing importance of effective communication in an "information society."

> If you're a history instructor, you might relate historical issues with governmental issues of today.

> If you teach science, your classes might take the "global perspective" and/or interweave local issues into the subject matter.

Throughout any course there are ways to establish relationships among book learning, critical thinking, and ways to improve your town, state, region, or country.

A quality instructor provides these kinds of assignments so that all students may develop. Not only do these connections motivate the naturally curious student, but they also draw the less motivated student into the assignment.

Students need to feel that they can make some contributions to the class. You can help by planning well and facilitating the activities. Students are most closely affected by your actions, which indeed speak louder than words.

You might use surveys to poll students for their opinions. Regular surveys (at least twice a semester) can make each student feel he or she is making an important contribution to the whole class.

Every student is unique and possesses special gifts. The quality instructor will begin the first day of class by determining what each student has to offer and will allow each the right to share that potential with the class. Students who feel that they are contributing in a variety of ways will be eager to participate and willing to help other students do quality work.

Improve Constantly

After determining the goals of the class and putting them into effect through teamwork and communication, you must strive for continuous improvement in your classroom. You can do this by observing and interacting with various students. Have students spend several minutes at the end of each class period or every week evaluating what they've done and what they need to do to increase their efficiency and improve the quality of their work.

Perhaps this is a matter of altering the flow of activities, moving the furniture, or providing a few additional minutes to let students discuss a matter with team members or classmates. This may involve moving students as well, but never through coercion or punishment. Feedback should provide necessary data to improve methods, materials, organization, and styles of presentation.

Constant improvement alerts students to the notion that they must become change-oriented. Indeed, changing the system of education means dramatic change for you as well. You must be a role-model of flexibility, adopting a change-orientation and teaching students to follow suit. This entire procedure allows students to become flexible with the learning process, permitting them to recognize ways to continually improve.

The following checksheet tool will help you baseline your **Human Resource Development and Management** skills. There are five subcategories. Circle the point next to the criterion that most nearly describes your present classroom situation.

What are your key strategies for increasing the effectiveness, productivity, and participation of *all* students?

Points	Criteria

1   I have no formal strategy.

2   My strategy is dependent on the course content.

3   I have a formal and flexible strategy that encourages students to participate in assessing the classroom climate and offer suggestions for improving it. I empower students to work for the success of all.

4   My classroom environment is completely without fear, and cooperative learning opportunities are essential parts of each class period. All of my students share in the success of the group.

5   I assume the role of a quality instructor, challenging my students to tap their potential. My students evaluate the quality of their own work as well as the work of others, offering suggestions and encouragement.

Please describe how you educate students in quality improvement.

Points   Criteria

1   My students receive no education in the principles of TQM.

2   I teach students about TQM techniques that apply to immediate subject matter skills.

3   I teach my students about the principles of TQM.

4   I teach my students about the principles and processes of quality, including the Plan-Do-Check-Act cycle. The students use these principles in their daily work.

5   Learning in my classroom is based on the continuous improvement of *all* students as the key to success.

What percentage of your current students have ever received education in quality improvement concepts and processes?

Points   Criteria

1   0%

2   Less than 25%

3   25% to 60%

4   61% to 90%

5   91% to 100%

Describe how you positively reinforce student contributions to quality improvement (*e.g.*, recognition of teams, awards).

Points   Criteria

1 Traditional grades are my reward for achievement.

2 I give typical performance reviews focusing on individual efforts.

3 I give commendations and other rewards as I deem appropriate.

4 I give commendations and other rewards as my students and I deem appropriate.

5 I base team recognition and incentives for efforts to improve the processes and systems. My role is to support and facilitate the efforts of the team. I post information about team rewards. I have a system in place for distributing information to parents, community members, and colleagues.

What have you done to ensure the quality of the environment in your classroom? How have you made it more supportive? How have you empowered students to actively participate in the learning process? If you have examples, please include them.

Points   Criteria

1 My classroom environment reflects an attitude of: be quiet, do your work, and don't question or make suggestions.

2 I consider and discuss administration's suggestions.

3   I discuss some student suggestions and ideas with my class.

4   I use a participation management approach, in which I encourage students to make suggestions, discuss options, and collaborate with others to implement group decisions.

5   I use an inverted pyramid, in which my role is to be a leader and to support quality work. My students are performing that work — adhocracy at its best.

Chapter Five: Information and Analysis

"Knowledge is the only instrument of production that is not subject to diminishing returns."

J.M. Clark
Journal of Political Economy (October 1927)

In order to identify problem areas in your instructional system, you need to examine the scope, validity, use, and management of data and information that underlie your classroom process. You must examine adequate data and information to support a prevention-based quality approach using "management by fact."

Take time to briefly consider the following before reading this chapter and answering the questions on the subsequent checksheet:

> List the areas in which you have data to illustrate quality trends by function and/or process in your classroom (materials, student satisfaction, student involvement, employer satisfaction, number of students entering graduate school, students adequately prepared for the next level of instruction in any given curricular area, student retention, time for achieving mastery in any curricular area, etc.). Include examples of quality trends.

Why Statistics?

Data collection is the foundation for effective leadership. Statistical data, in combination with human relations, can help you uncover clues as to how your class is performing.

Data helps you track not only your students' performance, but your own. You can use data to improve how you teach and how your students learn.

You may want to look at areas that need attention but are difficult for you to understand. For instance, a certain group of students may be performing at levels lower than you anticipated. Or maybe you feel less comfortable with a particular group of students.

Try looking at a given situation from a different point of view. Can you imagine it? Try to determine which systems and processes are weak. This is just one area where factual, statistical data becomes very important.

There are many kinds of data that you can collect and use for baseline information. The statistical data you select for analysis will in part be determined by the academic level of your courses.

Another factor critical to data selection will be an analysis of your **customers**.

Before collecting any data, you'll need to:

- Establish a small group of students and colleagues who are directly involved in the area in question. The group can assist in the data collection to determine root causes of problems and create action plans.
- Decide which problems need to be addressed.
- State the problems clearly and succinctly. Be certain to include when and where they occur, and to what extent.
- Establish a chart that diagrams the exact breakdown points leading to the problems.
- Agree on the causes of the problems.
- Develop an action plan to improve the processes and resolve the problems.
- Implement the action plan and monitor the results.

Sometimes it's obvious what the principal problems of a given class are and why you need to address them. In most cases, however, a major system that inhibits quality within a unit may not be readily apparent either to you or to most of the students in your class. Some instructors, for example, say that their classroom has so many poorly prepared students that they don't know where to begin.

In order to concentrate on the major problems that detract from quality work, it may become necessary for you to have each class identify the major problems, using one or more of the tools listed in Table 5.1. The actual procedures for using these tools are explained in Chapters 7 and 8.

Table 5.1 Tools to identify and rank problem processes and/or systems

Affinity Diagram
- Used to examine problems that are complex
- Used to build team consensus
- Results can be used with **Relations Diagram**

Cause-and-Effect Diagram (Fishbone)
- Used to identify root causes of a problem
- Used to draw out many ideas about causes

Flow Chart
- Gives a picture of the processes in the system

Force Field Analysis
- Used when changing the system might be difficult

Histogram
- Bar graph that gives info. about data set and shape
- Used to predict the stability of the system

Nominal Group Process
- Structured process that helps groups make decisions
- Useful in choosing a problem to work on
- Used to build team consensus
- Used to draw out many ideas about causes

Pareto Diagram
- Bar chart that ranks data by categories
- Used to show how a few problems contribute to overall problems

Relations Diagram
- Helps team analyze cause-and-effect relationships
- Directs the team to the **root** causes of problems

Systematic Diagram
- Used when broad goal is focus of team's work
- Used with **Affinity Diagram** or **Relations Diagram**
- Used when action plan to accomplish goal is complex

Case Study

An Economics 100 instructor had his students use the Nominal Group Process (NGP) to identify and rank the major problems that inhibited their learning.

The instructor started by explaining to the class why he was concerned, what the essential problem was, and what he hoped to accomplish by using this technique. He respected the students and was willing to work to establish trust with each of them. Had only some of the students participated (either the achievers or the non-achievers), the results would have been invalid. Therefore, it was imperative for the instructor to lay the proper groundwork before beginning the NGP.

In fact, the instructor decided that someone other than he should be in charge of facilitating the process. He chose an average student who was fairly well-liked by the other students. This helped students feel comfortable about expressing their perceptions.

The instructor stated his concerns to the class as factually and non-judgmentally as possible. He then asked the students to give their impressions of why student performance was so poor in his class.

The instructor was very careful to listen respectfully to the students. He didn't become defensive. By the time the students had finished talking, the facilitator had developed a list of responses, as shown in Table 5.2.

Table 5.2 Rank and final values of perceived problems as assigned by students using the NGP

Rank	Perceived Problem	Final Value
1	The class is repetitious	280
2	The class is boring	230
3	The class is not important	180
4	The class is not challenging	20
5	Others	90
	TOTAL	800

This technique, like other TQM techniques, won't work unless your students feel they are operating in a non-punitive environment. Students who believe in your sincerity to alter the class so that they can reach greater levels of achievement will want to help you in this process. But students who feel threatened by possible reprisals from you or other students will be less apt to be honest and will not provide you with the information you need.

So it's very important that you explain your intentions, why you decided to do this, and how committed you are to make positive change. (Of course, you should already have posted your mission statement and spoken to your students about TQM.)

Let's follow the problems listed above to demonstrate how various TQM tools were used to solve this "systems" problem.

Using results from the NGP, the instructor and the students agreed to establish an action team to concentrate on improving success and making the class more fun. After consulting with the students, the instructor established a team consisting of seven students, himself, and two people from local businesses. The team was to make specific recommendations to improve the learning system in the class.

They began by flow charting the learning system (see Figure 5.1 on the next page).

Figure 5.1 Flow chart of testing system in Economics 100

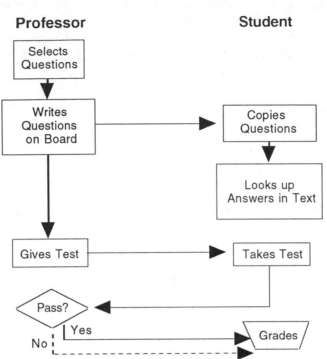

As you can see, there is no feedback loop for students who fail the test. At the end of each week, there are many students who have not learned the materials, defeating the instructor's goal.

The process breaks down because there is only a one-way flow. Students who don't pass simply fail. There is no opportunity for them to rectify mistakes or become engaged in the process differently.

If the flow was different, the team concluded, students might be more successful.

On the basis of the results, the team decided to get additional information about the root causes of the unacceptably low student achievement rate. The action team posted a Fishbone (Cause-and-Effect) Diagram and invited students to add their remarks (Figure 5.2).

Figure 5.2 Fishbone Diagram

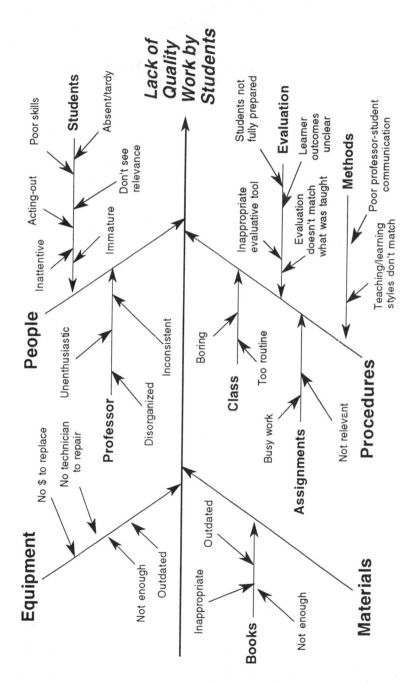

As a result of the data from these TQM tools, the action team recommended changes in the "system." The instructor then revised the system based on the team's recommendations (Figure 5.3).

Figure 5.3 Revised flow chart of testing system in Economics 100

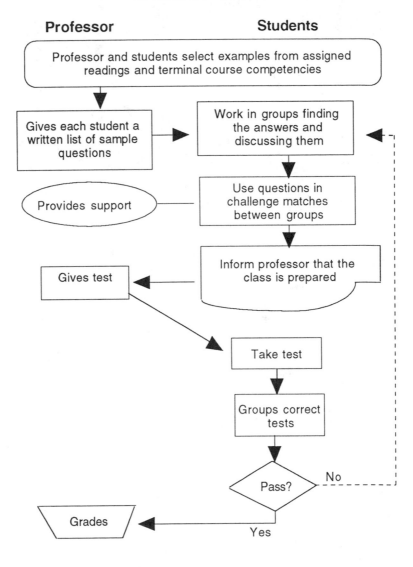

After the system was modified, the instructor compared and posted Run Charts of the percent of students in the class who received a grade of 90% or better on the quizzes before and after the system changes (Figure 5.4). (Students were also encouraged to record their personal scores so that they could determine their best manner for learning.)

The instructor kept information on each student and found it to be very useful in determining individual learning styles.

Figure 5.4 Run Chart for Economics 100

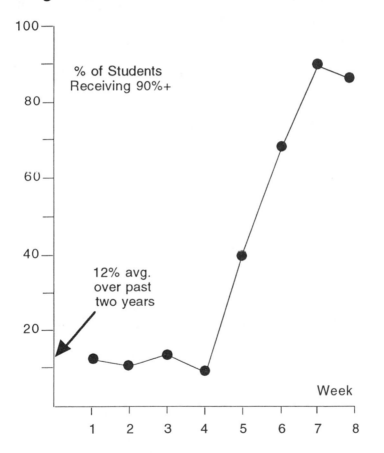

Other Considerations

You can use data obtained from whatever standardized tests are administered on your campus. This data can be very useful when assessing students' ability to be successful at the next level of education. Although you'll be sifting through data from the previous year's students, the trends you spot can give you clues about potential problem areas within your classes.

Attendance records are another source of valuable data. Graphing or charting absences along with such things as achievement will give you insight on the resulting effects.

You may also want to gather data on the length of time students take to learn the material. In outcomes-based education models, students are generally allowed to proceed at their own pace until they have achieved mastery at a level determined by each instructor. Some campuses, like Governors State University (IL) when it used a competency-based model, have recorded this data and determined the length of time it takes most students to achieve mastery. The campuses use this information for determining the length of time per unit.

It's important to recognize, however, that each of us needs a certain amount of stress in our lives. Without it, we would be so bored that we would be unable to complete our work. With students, there's a fine balance between pushing too much and not demanding enough.

If you work with graduating seniors, it's important for you to determine the satisfaction levels of both graduate schools and major employers. One way to do this is to obtain information on which graduate schools have accepted your students.

Have any of your students taken the MCAT test, the NLN test, or a similar test? If so, how did they do? What does the trend look like?

Survey the students after the first year of graduate school to see how many are successful. If they're having difficulty, try to discover what you could have been done differently that would have helped. This information will provide data for re-evaluating the curriculum and selecting materials for your course.

You can survey employers to discover what skills they require for entry-level employment. In some positions, for example, students need a basic knowledge of computer software. In fact, most larger employers in a given region seem to prefer similar

74

software. Students are at a disadvantage when seeking employment if your institution doesn't have this dominant software. Knowing this information gives you an opportunity to ask your institution to buy software. If that isn't feasible, perhaps you could ask local employers using the software to buy a copy for the college.

These are examples of the kinds of data you can obtain and utilize to determine the success of students and your teaching techniques. You should use every piece of data to its fullest because:

- no one wants to provide information if you won't use it,
- you should analyze and provide information to your customers, including students, parents, colleagues, and the institution's governing board,
- the only reason to collect information is to use it to alter the processes and systems within your classroom,
- you should disseminate information to students and employers, allowing them to become partners in change so that everyone can become a winner, and
- the information becomes part of the Plan-Do-Check-Act Cycle which is crucial to TQM.

Information should become your friend. It will give you focus for change. It will allow you to plan effectively and make necessary changes.

Once you have planned and changed a process or system, the *do* part of the cycle kicks in. After you gather additional information, which is the *check* stage, you can then *act* (or change again, if necessary).

The cycle continues for you and your students every day, all year. It's the process by which you seek constant improvement.

The following is a checksheet tool that will help you baseline your **Information and Analysis** skills. There is one subcategory. Circle the point next to the criterion that most nearly describes your present classroom situation.

List the areas in which you have data to illustrate quality trends by function and/or process in your classroom (materials, student satisfaction, student involvement, employer satisfaction, number of students entering graduate school, students adequately prepared for the next level of instruction in any given curricular area, student retention, time for achieving mastery in any curricular area, etc.). Include examples of quality trends.

Points	Criteria

1   I have no data or only the standard evaluation data.

2   I have standard retention data and some information on curricular trends.

3   I use statistical methods to monitor critical processes and systems.

4   I collect quality analysis data and make it available for all (including students) to examine.

5   I use statistical data to analyze classroom processes and systems. I use the P-D-C-A Cycle to improve the classroom's processes and systems.

Chapter Six: Quality and Operational Results

"Every job is a self-portrait of the person who did it. Autograph your work with excellence."

Anonymous

Quality improvement should be based upon objective measures derived from analysis of customer requirements/expectations and operations and examination of current quality levels in relation to those of competing institutions. To assess yourself, complete the following tasks:

Present in graph form some key improvement data on your students.

Briefly describe one or two continuous improvement projects that have led to the results presented above.

Describe how you compare your courses with other courses within or outside your discipline (benchmarking).

As you and your students work to improve the classroom, you must consider certain things:

- Standardized test scores may ignore other, more important measures of knowledge.
- In tackling the barriers to student knowledge, you should work on one or two problems at a time, rather than on many.

Standardized tests will never be the best way to measure student achievement in developing critical thinking skills or problem-solving. Depending on standardized tests limits your thinking about learning. Worse, the results are often used to punish students, instructors, and educational systems. In the TQM approach, you must build quality into the process. Use inspection only if it provides information leading to continuous improvement.

Outcomes-based education is one tool you can use to end dependence on inspection. It allows both you and your students to focus on the process of learning. You give a test only when you're reasonably sure, from the results of other classroom work and assignments, that students have clearly acquired the desired knowledge. Students who do not achieve mastery will require additional work to thoroughly learn the material. No matter how many times a student takes the test, the only grade he or she will eventually receive is one indicating mastery.

In his book, *The Eternally Successful Organization* (1988, p. 191), Crosby says, "Performance reviews probably do more to make employees antagonistic to their company than any other single item."

One of the problems with traditional methods of evaluating teaching effectiveness is that most are based solely on classroom observation. You should supplement observation with data to provide classroom insights in an efficient, effective, ongoing data collection process.

It's important to remember, as you collect and graph such data, trends indicating the development of another area for improvement.

Many good instructors become defensive or angry when they get one or two suggestions for improvement from the dean or a colleague. Clearly, this response suggests that the institutional evaluation system is based on fear.

Deming (*Out of the Crisis*, 1982, pp. 109-110) says:

> A common fallacy is the supposition that it is possible to rate people, to put them in rank order of performance for next year, based on performance last year.
>
> The performance of anybody is the result of a combination of many forces — the person himself, the people that he works with, the job, the materials that he works on, his equipment, his customers, his management, his supervision, and environmental conditions in the workplace. These forces will produce unbelievably large differences between people. In fact, ... apparent differences between people arise almost entirely from action of the system that they work in, not from the people themselves.

Gradual Improvement

You should direct continuous improvement projects toward one or two areas in your class. If you try to change too many things at once, you'll make it impossible to be certain about effects and causes.

As you collect data, your action team may decide to make other changes, based on new information. Be careful: a systematic, slow approach will work better than a shotgun approach. Patience will be key to your success. So avoid the "fool's gold" of quick fixes.

Continuously remind yourself, "Everyone makes changes, but very few take care to inject them into the bloodstream of the company" (Crosby, *The Eternally Successful Organization*, 1988, p.120). To prevent a problem from recurring, make changes only after assessing your data. Take a methodical approach — the data will demonstrate whether changes in classroom processes and systems have produced the desired results.

There are endless ways for you to involve the students in continuous improvement. Remember that your class is a team working together to:

- determine the quality improvement project,
- include everyone in the transformation, and
- systematically collect and report data so that everyone knows the outcomes.

To create a "total quality classroom," it's crucial for you to benchmark your class with a "world class" classroom. Take the best of several classrooms and capitalize on the strengths of each to make significant improvements in your classroom. Benchmarking against the very best will help you realize the potential for students as well as the challenges you and your students must face.

By leading your class through the continuous improvement process, driving out fear, and empowering your students, you can realize greater achievement than you've ever imagined. Maintain high expectations, then work toward improving your systems and processes so that everyone can fulfill them. Continuous self-evaluation is not a luxury. It's vital to the goal of higher education.

The following checksheet tool will help you baseline your **Quality and Operational Results** skills. There are three subcategories. Circle the point next to the criterion that most nearly describes your present classroom situation.

Present in graph form some key data on student improvement in your class.

Points	Criteria

1   I don't have any graphs.

2   I use traditional quality indicator information (*e.g.*, grades).

3   I evaluate traditional information in class, using graphs that students understand.

4   I gather field intelligence data and evaluate it in graphic form (*e.g.*, the number or percentage of students passing professional certification tests, enrolling in graduate schools, or being employed by a Fortune 500 company).

5   I regularly use information related to strategic quality objectives and post it in graphic form in the classroom. I provide reports to our governing board, administration, and employers.

Briefly describe one or two continuous improvement projects that have led to the results presented above.

Points	Criteria

1   I have no project groups or measurable results.

2   I form project groups quickly, putting effort into the nature of the project and how it might lead to quality improvement.

3   I use mastery learning and chart the results, but use cooperative learning only occasionally.

4   I establish project groups with assignments that are cross-curricular, global, and meaningful.

5   My students are engaged in project groups that study issues. The result is cross-curricular, global, and meaningful work. I serve as a supportive leader; my students do the work, using quality methods and tools.

Describe how you compare your courses with other courses within or outside your discipline (benchmarking).

Points   Criteria

1   I have no comparable data.

2   I use standard accounting information, such as standardized test scores and the number of students passing.

3   I collect and analyze data from outside sources, such as employers and former students.

4   I benchmark against competitors, comparing percentages of students going on to graduate school.

5   I use an active program to obtain benchmarking data on all functions and services from the *best* in those areas, whether they are competitors, departments, or institutions.

Chapter Seven: Assessing the Situation

"Assessment would be very different if college teaching were viewed as an ongoing reciprocity among students, instructors, and materials, a collaborative venture with shared responsibility for what goes into a class and what comes out of it.

Evaluation would be built into the daily routine. Participants would often ask and answer questions such as:

'What did we intend to do today?
How did we go about it?
What helped or hindered our progress?
How can we do it better?
Do our goals need redefining?
Is everyone getting a fair chance to learn?
Is everyone carrying his/her weight?'"

Rachel M. Lauer, Director, Straus Thinking and Learning Center, Pace University, in *The Chronicle of Higher Education*, Sept. 8, 1993, p. B4

Once you understand the principles of TQM, you may want to start applying it to problems in your classroom.

Most problem-solving involves several steps:

- realizing that a problem exists,
- forming a team to study the situation,
- gathering input from team,
- collecting data,
- representing and analyzing the data,
- proposing action, and
- assessing the impact of changes.

In this chapter, we'll use TQM tools to identify problems and collect data in several situations. In Chapter 8, we'll use other TQM tools to proceed through the remaining steps of the problem-solving process outlined above.

Let's consider five situations:

- How would Professor Jones analyze the flow of class assignments and use TQM tools to identify learning projects that would enhance his sociology classes?
- How would Professor Appleton's introductory biology students analyze the relationship between their study habits and their grades?
- How would Professor Wright use TQM tools to determine why her algebra students don't finish their homework?
- How would Professor Stone, a drama instructor, establish a set design and construction shop?
- How would Professor Salmon determine the amount of time it takes for her English students to master the material?

After realizing their situations and forming teams to get input, each of these people would identify their problems and collect data. We'll explain how you, too, can use different TQM tools to achieve similar ends.

87

Operational Definition

An operational definition states process expectations for every process to be improved. Many troubles within the classroom stem from imprecise or undefined operational definitions. So before you collect data, you must clearly understand this important concept.

Use operational definitions for **every** process you want to improve. If conditions change (*e.g.,* student motivation increases), the operational definition may change as well.

Procedure

1. State the problem

Before you examine any characteristic of a system or process, define the actual problem or issue in the form of a question. For example, a nursing instructor might ask, "How can I increase the success rate of my students in identifying muscles and bones in the body?"

2. Identify the criterion to be applied to the object or the group

In our example, the criterion to be measured is the success rate of nursing students in identifying the muscles and bones of the body. The students have previously been taught all major bones and muscles. They have participated in a variety of exercises using different instructional modes. There have been group activities utilizing the skeleton and cadaver.

3. Identify the test

Define the actual testing method and evaluation procedure. In our example, the student identifies the major bones of the body from numbered bones on a skeleton, then names and identifies the major muscles on a labeled cadaver. Students may leave their seats and examine the specimens closely.

4. Describe the decision process

The decision process allows you to confirm or deny success. In this example, students assess each other's answers using a scoresheet that each discussion group has developed and checked against a master sheet.

Flow Charts

Although the flow chart is one of the most useful tools in TQM, it is also probably the most underutilized. Flow charting is a way to get a snapshot of each process in a system. A flow chart can demonstrate where non-value-added work is being performed. Non-value-added work adds to the cost of doing business.

After you draw a flow chart and identify redundant processes, a team can easily generate a different flow chart showing how the processes in the system should be structured.

There are many types of flow charts, but we will describe two useful in academic units: the Deployment and Process flow charts.

Deployment Flow Chart Procedure

1. Define the system

Each system consists of a series of processes. However, it isn't always clear where one system ends and another begins, since many systems involve more than one process. So your team should agree on the starting and ending points it wish to study.

As with any universal visual tool, flow charting has a set of standardized symbols (Myron Tribus, 1989), as shown below:

Figure 7.1 Flowchart symbols

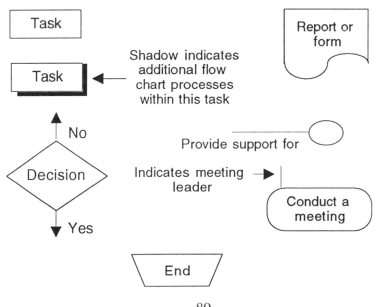

2. Draw the chart

A deployment flow chart shows interrelationships between people and the tasks they perform while working within a system to generate service or products.

The members of your team should walk through each step in the system they are studying. As they do, they should have the people performing each task describe what is actually involved. Team members should take copious notes. Only after doing this should they draw the deployment flow chart.

Flow charts should not be drawn only when there are problems in a system. Instead, draw them for every task and process in every system to root out non-value-added work. And if there are any changes within a system, update its flow chart immediately for all to see.

In the example below, we'll follow an actual deployment flow chart of a sociology class assignment initiated by Dr. Jones.

The first thing to do in preparing a deployment flow chart is to enter the "people" coordinate horizontally. The boxes can contain either the particular person or his or her position or the particular department/unit that is performing a task.

Figure 7.2 Starting the deployment flow chart

Instructor	Group/Team	Student

Next, list the tasks and/or major steps.

Figure 7.3 Steps for the deployment flow chart

1. Prepare assignment (instructor)

2. Determine options (instructor and group)

3. Analyze options and select preferred one (group)

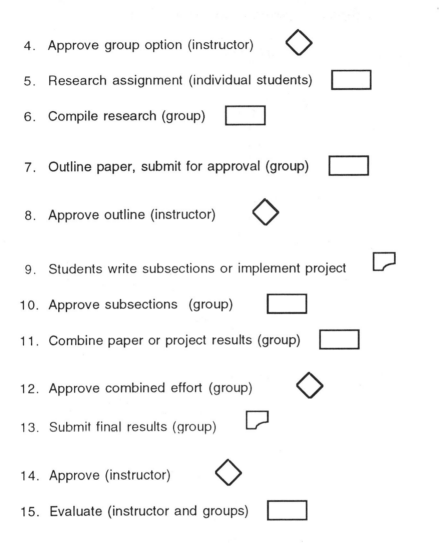

4. Approve group option (instructor)

5. Research assignment (individual students)

6. Compile research (group)

7. Outline paper, submit for approval (group)

8. Approve outline (instructor)

9. Students write subsections or implement project

10. Approve subsections (group)

11. Combine paper or project results (group)

12. Approve combined effort (group)

13. Submit final results (group)

14. Approve (instructor)

15. Evaluate (instructor and groups)

Using the symbols described above, draw the flow chart, as shown on the next page.

Figure 7.4 Deployment flow chart

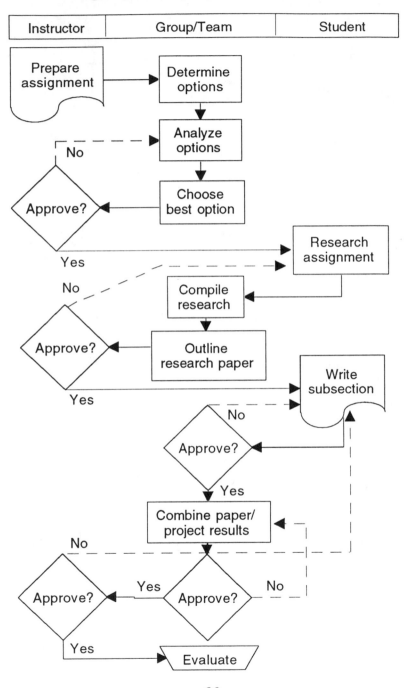

3. Record and discuss the results

Examine the lines and determine if there is any non-value-added work that you can reduce or eliminate. If there appears to be a breakdown in the system — if someone is not supplying his or her customer with quality work — try to examine the reason(s) why. Are there barriers or decision-making delays that slow the flow?

After examining the system above, a team recommended the revision shown on the next page. The new system reduced the inspection time and empowered students to make decisions about the work quality of their classmates. As a result, students worked harder, assignments were completed faster, and the results were excellent.

Figure 7.5 Revised deployment flow chart

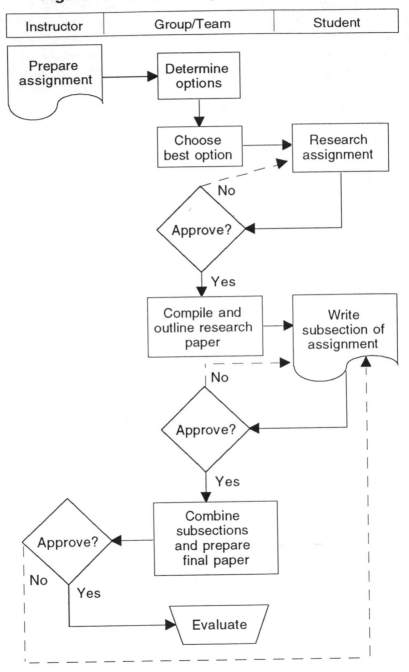

Process Flow Chart Procedure

1. State the problem

The process flow chart shows the major steps in a system. It doesn't attempt to demonstrate the interrelationships among people doing tasks. As with any flow chart, the team should agree to the starting and ending points of the system it wants to study.

2. Draw the chart

The members of the classroom team should walk through each step in the system they are studying. As they do, they should have the people performing each task describe what is actually involved. They should also take copious notes and draw sketches.

The team should list the major steps in the system, and then, using the standardized symbols below, draw the flow chart.

Figure 7.6 Symbols for the process flow chart

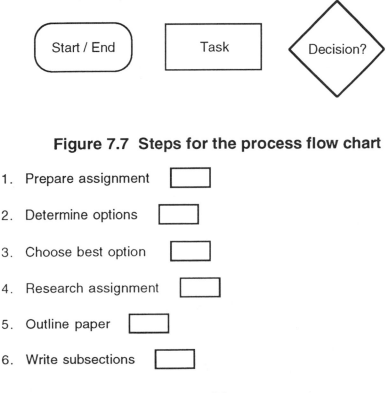

Figure 7.7 Steps for the process flow chart

1. Prepare assignment

2. Determine options

3. Choose best option

4. Research assignment

5. Outline paper

6. Write subsections

7. Prepare final paper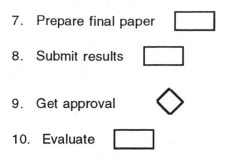

8. Submit results

9. Get approval

10. Evaluate

Figure 7.8 Process flow chart

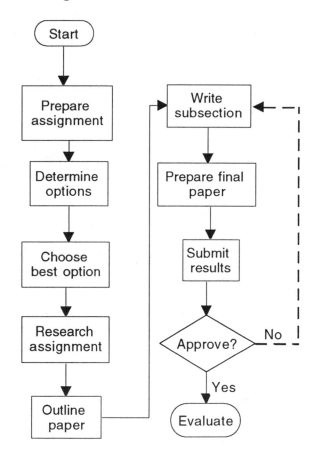

3. Record and discuss the results

By studying the chart, the team members may be able to recommend ways to reduce redundant steps and improve the processes of the classroom system.

Nominal Group Process

This technique can help you identify and rank major strengths and weaknesses of a department/unit/institution, and give each participant an equal voice.

For the nominal group process (NGP), each group of students should have a facilitator (usually the instructor), who acts as a moderator. The facilitator may encourage some members of each team who are reluctant to participate; likewise, the facilitator may restrain members who normally try to control such processes. All members need to feel comfortable with the process and participating in it.

Each facilitator will need to have a stopwatch to use during the workshop.

Each group should consist of five to 10 people. Since large classrooms will have several groups, it's possible that each group may perceive different problems/weaknesses. If this should happen, the facilitator may have to review the results and plan another session for the entire group before assigning final rankings.

The following example is also from Dr. Jones' sociology class. Dr. Jones called the session because of his concerns about student development in the classroom. Students, a representative number of alumni, and Dr. Jones arrived at a consensus about the perceived problems and/or weaknesses that inhibited development.

Procedure

1. Introduce the process (five minutes)

The facilitator gives instructions for the process but does not influence the group's decisions. He or she keeps the group working within the time limits.

The facilitator tells the participants that the NGP allows them to explore areas systematically and arrive at a consensus. The process consists of developing a list and ranking perceived problems. The participants discuss the results and identify the perceived problems that are the most important to the group.

2. Present the question (15 minutes)

The facilitator directs the question for the group to consider. For example, the facilitator might ask, "What do you think are the major problems that inhibit quality in your classroom?"

The facilitator repeats the question and asks each participant to write three- to five-word answers for each perceived problem **Form A** (see below). The facilitator then asks each member to complete Form A silently and independently, and reminds participants that they have five minutes for this task. At the end of five minutes, if it appears that several members have not finished, the facilitator states that he or she will allow two additional minutes.

Form A   Listing of perceived problems

What do you think are the major problems that inhibit quality in your unit? Please use the form below and write out short but specific answers.

Item #	Perceived Problem
1	
2	
3	
4	
5	

3. Develop a Master List (20 Minutes)

While the participants are listing perceived problems, the facilitator uses an overhead and projects Chart I (shown below).

At the end of the time allotted for listing perceived problems, the facilitator asks the participants to stop writing. Then the facilitator asks each to read aloud one of the perceived problems on his or her list. The facilitator tells the participants that if they come to a problem on their list that has been given, they need not repeat it.

If several items appear to be the same, the facilitator asks the group members to vote on whether they think the items are the same. If a majority feels the items are the same, the perceived problem isn't listed again; if not, both items are listed.

There is **no discussion** of the list at this point. For a period of time, the participants are not influenced by the opinions of others.

As each perceived problem is given, the facilitator records the item on the Chart I. He or she must **not** suggest categories or combinations. He or she simply numbers and records the items as presented by the participants (unless the item is too long, in which case the facilitator tries to shorten the phrasing without changing the meaning). If, at the end of 20 minutes, some items haven't been presented, the facilitator asks each member to give the one **most important** perceived problem remaining on his or her list.

A sample of the perceived problems that resulted from the NGP in Dr. Jones' sociology class is shown below.

Chart I Perceived problems that inhibit quality in Dr. Jones' sociology class

Item #	Perceived Problem	Init. Val.	Final Val.	Final Rank
1	Class size is too large			
2	Textbooks are out of date			
3	Classroom is in disrepair			
4	Students are tardy			
5	Too many students are absent			
6	Too many interruptions			
7	Class periods are too short			
8	Instructor is unenthusiastic			
9	Instructor hasn't kept up with new techniques & information			
10	Class activities are too routine			
11	Coercive, punitive discipline policy			
12	Students don't finish assignments			
13	Instructor coaches football & uses class time to talk to players			
14	Tests are too hard			

4. Clarify the master list items (15 minutes)

The facilitator points to each item on the master list, reads it aloud, and asks if everyone understands it. If not, he or she asks the individual who generated the item to clarify it.

The facilitator should **not** attempt to condense the list, nor permit the group to discuss the relative importance of the perceived problems.

Remember: the purpose of this step is **clarification.**

5. Rank the items (15 minutes)

The facilitator distributes copies of **Form B** (see below) and requests that each participant select and rank the **five** most important perceived problems. No. 5 is the most important, and No. 1 is the least important.

Form B Initial ranking of perceived problems

Please refer to the master list (Chart I) that describes the perceived problems and rank the five that you think are the most important.

Item Number from the Master List	Initial Subjective Ranking Value
	#5 (most important)
	#4
	#3
	#2
	#1 (least important)

The participants then record their rankings. The facilitator collects the forms and tallies the results on the master list, giving each item an initial score, as shown on the next page.

Chart I-a Perceived problems that inhibit quality in Dr. Jones' sociology class

Item #	Perceived Problem	Init. Val.	Final Val.	Final Rank
1	Class size is too large	7		
2	Textbooks are out of date	23		
3	Classroom is in disrepair	17		
4	Students are tardy	40		
5	Too many students are absent	20		
6	Too many interruptions	1		
7	Class periods are too short	3		
8	Instructor is unenthusiastic	29		
9	Instructor hasn't kept up with new techniques & information	31		
10	Class activities are too routine	45		
11	Coercive, punitive discipline policy	8		
12	Students don't finish assignments	30		
13	Instructor coaches football & uses class time to talk to players	27		
14	Tests are too hard	35		

6. Discuss initial ranking (30 minutes)

The facilitator asks the participants to discuss the results of the rankings. The participants may **elaborate, defend,** and **dispute** the rankings, but they can't add items.

The facilitator should remind participants that this is their opportunity to express opinions and persuade others. The facilitator attempts to prevent anyone from dominating, however.

At this point, similar items may be combined into a single category. In the example above, the 14 items were reduced to nine:

- Class size too large
- Textbooks are out of date
- Classroom is in disrepair
- Students are tardy
- Coercive, punitive discipline policy
- Students don't finish assignments
- Too many interruptions
- Class periods are too short
- Instructor is unenthusiastic

7. Break (20 minutes)

Some members of the group may find a break a welcome relief from the previous discussion or debate. Others may want to take the discussion into the hallway. The facilitator should have the participants return promptly after 20 minutes.

8. Do a final list and rank items (15 minutes)

After the items have been discussed, the facilitator should distribute a copy of **Form C** (see below) to all group members. He or she asks each member to rank the top five choices as before, from No. 5 to No. 1. At the end of the allotted time, the facilitator records the final values for each item on the master list.

Form C Final ranking of perceived problems

Please refer to the revised master list (Chart I-a) that describes the grouped perceived problems and rank the five that you think are most important.

Item Number from the Master List	Initial Subjective Ranking Value
	#5 (most important)
	#4
	#3
	#2
	#1 (least important)

The facilitator should record the final values and resulting ranks **Chart I-b** (see below). Dr. Jones' class obtained the following data, as shown on the next page.

102

Chart I-b Summary and rank of perceived problems that inhibit quality in Dr. Jones' sociology class

Item #	Perceived Problem	Init. Val.	Final Val.	Final Rank
1	Class size is too large	7	0	9
2	Textbooks are out of date	23	17	5
3	Classroom is in disrepair	17	2	7
4	Students are tardy	40	29	4
5	Too many students are absent	20	0	
6	Too many interruptions	1	32	3
7	Class periods are too short	3	5	6
8	Instructor is unenthusiastic	29	97	2
9	Instructor hasn't kept up with new techniques & information	31	0	
10	Class activities are too routine	45	0	
11	Coercive, punitive discipline policy	8	1	8
12	Students don't finish assignments	30	110	1
13	Instructor coaches football & uses class time to talk to players	27	0	
14	Tests are too hard	35	0	

On the following pages are the various charts and forms you'll need to conduct the NGP in your class.

Chart I Perceived problems inhibiting
quality in our class

Item #	Perceived Problem	Init. Val.	Final Val.	Final Rank
1				
2				
3				
4				
5				
6				
7				
8				
9				
10				
11				
12				
13				
n				

Form A Listing of perceived problems

What do you think are the major problems that inhibit quality in this class? Please use the form below and write out short but specific answers.

Item #	Perceived Problem
1	
2	
3	
4	
5	

Form B Initial ranking of perceived problems

Please refer to the master list (Chart I) that describes the perceived problems and rank which you think are the five major problems.

Item Number from the Master List	Initial Subjective Ranking Value
	#5 (most important)
	#4
	#3
	#2
	#1 (least important)

Form C Final ranking of perceived problems

Please refer to the revised master list (Chart I) that describes the grouped problems and indicate which you think are the five major problems.

Item Number from the Master List	Initial Subjective Ranking Value
	#5 (most important)
	#4
	#3
	#2
	#1 (least important)

Chart I (revised) Summary and rank of perceived problems that inhibit quality in our class

Item #	Perceived Problem	Init. Val.	Final Val.	Final Rank
1				
2				
3				
4				
5				
6				
7				
8				
9				
10				
11				
12				
13				
n				

Cause-and-Effect Diagram

The Cause-and-Effect Diagram (CED) was developed by Professor Kaoru Ishikawa in 1943, while he was president of the Musashi Institute of Technology (Japan). The CED was created to provide a visual representation of a series of complex and interrelated elements. It's also called a "fishbone," or Ishikawa, diagram.

A CED is useful for getting input regarding the root causes of a specific problem. You can use it in brainstorming sessions or to get input from an entire class or group, since it can be posted at various sites.

Use the CED alone, or with a Relations Diagram, Affinity Diagram, or a Nominal Group Process, to look at the root causes of a problem in different ways.

Procedure

1. State the problem

Identify a specific problem contributing to a non-quality result. In the following example, the question is why students are doing poorly in Dr. Appleton's introductory biology class. The problem is placed on the far right-hand side of an overhead, a sheet of paper, a flip chart, or butcher paper.

Figure 7.9 Stating the problem

2. Record the perceptions

After drawing the backbone and the box with the identified problem, add the primary causal category boxes — people, equipment, materials and procedures — (some also add "environment"). Then draw arrows to connect them to the backbone. This begins the CED.

Figure 7.10 Recording the perceptions

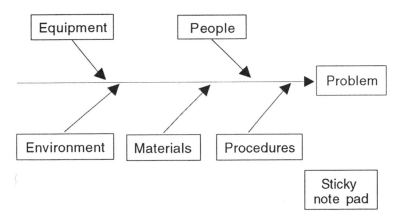

Provide sticky notepads so that participants can write one-word causes and sub-causes and place them in one of the primary causal categories. In some instances, you can add additional levels to sub-causes.

Figure 7.11 Adding causes and sub-causes

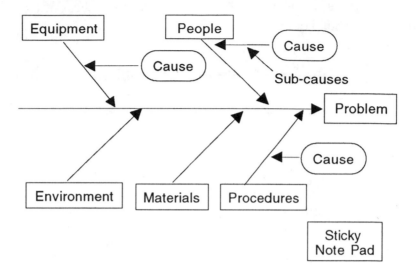

3. Complete the CED
    Shown on the next page is the completed CED, with the perceptions of Dr. Appleton's students as to why they are doing poorly in introductory biology.

Figure 7.12 Completed Cause and Effect Diagram

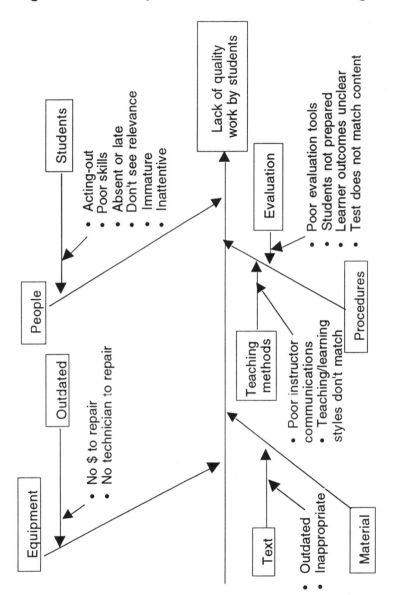

4. Record and discuss the results

Your purpose is to generate ideas about the probable causes of each problem and involve everyone in submitting suggestions. The group should not tolerate any criticism of any ideas. People should be able to build upon the causes and sub-causes posted by others.

5. Seek other suggestions

If someone identifies a major root cause for a problem, it couldbecome the focus of another fishbone diagram.

Affinity Diagram

The Affinity Diagram was invented by Jiro Kawakita, author of *A Scientific Exploration of Intellect* (1977). The Affinity Diagram organizes the issues concerning a process without quantification.

An Affinity Diagram is especially useful in clarifying a murky problem or issue. One benefit of using the Affinity Diagram at the very beginning of the TQM process is that it helps build consensus among team members studying a particular problem.

An Affinity Diagram can by itself identify the root causes of a problem. Or you can use the Scenario Builder, the Relations Diagram, or the Nominal Group Process. After identifying the root causes of a problem, you direct your efforts more efficiently.

Procedure

1. State the problem

Under the direction of a leader, the members of your team should arrive at a statement of the problem being addressed. For example: Dr. Jones' sociology class wants to include a volunteer community service project as part of the learning experience.

To work on the problem, the class forms a task force consisting of students, Jones, and members of several volunteer groups. The question they ask: What are the obstacles to including a community service project requirement in Dr. Jones' Sociology 303 course?

2. Record the perceptions

Each team member writes his or her perception on sticky note paper after announcing it to the group. The purpose of announcing the perception is to permit others to piggyback related ideas.

The process continues until people have exhausted their perceptions. The notes are placed on the wall or table.

Figure 7.13 Perceptions of team members

The dean won't permit it.

Students lack transportation.

Class periods are too short.

The department chair won't support it.

The vice president of academic affairs won't support it.

There is no need.

Other instructors won't support the idea and cooperate in flexible scheduling.

The liability of having students off campus is too great.

Organization members will find it too difficult to supervise the students.

Community service isn't perceived to be a student function.

Parents don't want students out of the classroom.

Students lack commitment.

Students aren't interested.

3. Group similar and/or related perceptions

The members of the team group similar cards or related perceptions. The grouped cards are said to have an "affinity" for

111

each other. The cards can be moved any number of times. It isn't uncommon to have 10 related groups, although there may be as few as three.

The perceptions listed above were grouped as follows:

Figure 7.14 Grouping of similar perceptions

Group 1

The dean won't permit it.

The vice president of academic affairs won't permit it.

The department chair won't support it.

Community service isn't perceived to be a student function.

The liability of having students   off campus is too great.

Group 2

There is no need.

Students aren't interested.

Students lack transportation.

Students lack commitment.

Group 3

> Parents don't want students
> out of the classroom.

Group 4

> Organization members will find
> it too difficult to supervise
> the students.

> Parents don't want students
> out of the classroom.

> Other instructors won't support
> the idea and cooperate
> in flexible scheduling.

> Class periods are too short.

4. Assign a name, with a header designation, to each group

The leader should read all of the perceptions in each group, and the members should agree to a name that can be assigned to each of the groups. The leader then writes a header card for each group.

If there is a miscellaneous group, the team should examine each perception and, if possible, place each card into one of the groups. If not, it is acceptable to have a group named "miscellaneous."

This stage of the process results in the following four header groups (as shown on the following pages):

113

Figure 7.15 Assigning names to each group

Group 1: The Administration

The dean won't permit it.

The vice president of academic affairs won't permit it.

The department chair won't support it.

Community service isn't perceived to be a student function.

The liability of having students off campus is too great.

Group 2: The Students

There is no need.

Students aren't interested.

Students lack transportation.

Students lack commitment.

Group 3: The Parents

Parents don't want students out of the classroom.

Group 4: The Faculty

Organization members will find it too difficult to supervise the students.

Parents don't want students out of the classroom.

Other instructors won't support the idea and cooperate in flexible scheduling.

Class periods are too short.

5. Draw the diagram

The team members should tape the papers or cards in each group onto a board or large flip chart. With the header cards at the top, the leader should draw borders around each group. The figure on the next page shows the completed Affinity Diagram.

Figure 7.16 Affinity Diagram — obstacles to establishing a service experience for sociology

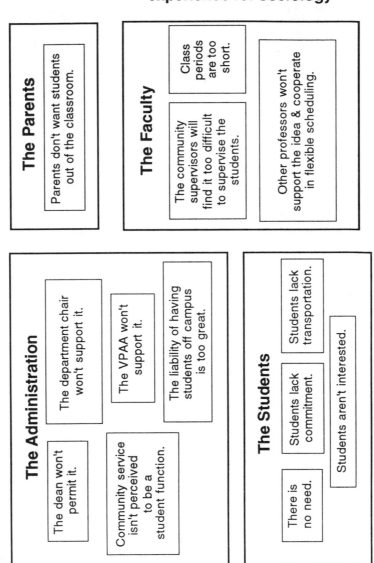

The Parents

Parents don't want students out of the classroom.

The Faculty

Class periods are too short.

The community supervisors will find it too difficult to supervise the students.

Other professors won't support the idea & cooperate in flexible scheduling.

The Administration

The department chair won't support it.

The VPAA won't support it.

The liability of having students off campus is too great.

The dean won't permit it.

Community service isn't perceived to be a student function.

The Students

Students lack transportation.

Students lack commitment.

Students aren't interested.

There is no need.

6. Discuss each group

Team members should discuss each group of factors and how the factors relate to the problem. This will result in a better understanding of the problem.

In order to arrive at a deeper understanding of each root cause, the team may want to use a Relations Diagram for each of the groups. Depending upon the problem or issue, the Scenario Builder, the Systematic Diagram, and the Cause-and-Effect Diagram may also be of value.

Force Field Analysis

The Force Field Analysis tool was the product of federally funded research to change the meat-buying habits of American housewives during World War II. It was invented by Professor Kurt Lewin of the University of Iowa.

Force Field Analysis identifies the perceived driving and restraining forces that affect a recommended change. Then, by increasing the forces driving the change, decreasing the forces inhibiting the change, or both, a team can recommend actions to bring the change about successfully.

The Force Field Analysis is much more useful when used with other TQM tools (*e.g.*, Nominal Group Process, Affinity Diagram, Scenario Builder.) This is especially true if the recommended change is counter to the "tradition" of the classroom.

The Force Field Analysis involves the use of brainstorming procedures. You select a facilitator, so that team members have equal opportunities to express their ideas without criticism. It encourages participants to build upon the ideas of others.

Procedure

1. State the problem

Under the direction of the team leader (the facilitator), the members of the team should arrive at a statement of the precise change desired. To do so, it may be necessary to use other TQM tools, such as the Nominal Group Process and the Affinity Diagram.

For example, Dr. Wright teaches algebra at a traditional university. She had heard from an instructor at another school that learning community concepts represented an effective teaching technique. She wanted her class to participate in one of the learning

117

community models. But she realized there were some potential problems, so she established a team to analyze the feasibility of such a change.

2. Record the suggestions

After brainstorming on the driving and restraining forces, much like the procedure for the NGP, the team — consisting of Wright, former students, other participating instructors, and the dean — recorded the following perceived driving and restraining forces:

Figure 7.17 Force Field Analysis driving and restraining forces

Recommended change: infuse learning community concepts into classroom	
Driving Forces (+)	Restraining Forces (−)
	Alters the curriculum
Students respond to this approach enthusiastically	Instructor isn't knowledgeable about learning communities
	Requires the instructor to think about the curriculum differently and plan alternative activities
Interrelates many aspects of the curriculum	Instructor lacks the skill to create instructional materials for all learning community courses
	No incentive for instructors to try new ideas in their classes
Accommodates many different learning styles	School lacks resources for instruction materials

3. Discuss and prioritize the driving and restraining forces

Each person who generates an idea should say why he or she feels it is important. Team members should then discuss each point.

After grouping the driving and restraining forces, the team should assign a value of importance to each point. For example, there are six items listed as restraining forces. Therefore, the team may wish to use the NGP technique and assign No. 5 to the most important perceived restraining force, No. 4 to the second most important, and so on, as shown below:

Figure 7.18 Force Field Analysis ranking values

Recommended change: infuse learning community concepts into classroom	
Driving Forces (+)	**Restraining Forces (−)**
	Alters the curriculum (-5)
Students respond to this approach enthusiastically (+1)	Instructor isn't knowledgeable about learning communities (-1)
	Requires the instructor to think about the curriculum differently and plan alternative activities (-4)
Interrelates many aspects of the curriculum (+3)	Instructor lacks the skill to create instructional materials for all learning community courses (-6)
	No incentive for instructors to try new ideas in their classes (-2)
Accommodates many different learning styles (+2)	School lacks resources for instruction materials (-3)

4. Recommendation steps

After recording, discussing, and prioritizing the driving and restraining forces, the team should begin to recommend steps to effect the desired change, as shown on the next page:

Figure 7.19 Force Field Analysis with recommendations

Recommended change: infuse learning community concepts into classroom	
Driving Forces (+)	**Restraining Forces (–)**
	Alters the curriculum (-5)
Students respond to this approach enthusiastically (+1)	Instructor isn't knowledgeable about learning communities (-1)
	Requires the instructor to think about the curriculum differently and plan alternative activities (-4)
Interrelates many aspects of the curriculum (+3)	Instructor lacks the skill to create instructional materials for all learning community courses (-6)
	No incentive for instructors to try new ideas in their classes (-2)
Accommodates many different learning styles (+2)	School lacks resources for instruction materials (-3)

Recommended actions:

1. The dean should provide funding for the instructors to attend a workshop on learning communities. (This would address the No. 1-, 4-, 5-, and 6-ranked restraining forces and the No. 2- and 3-ranked driving forces.)

2. This instructor should implement learning communities and present her plans and outcomes to the department faculty. (This would address the No. 2- and 5-ranked restraining forces and all the driving forces.)

3. Instructors who share their learning community plans will receive money from the Innovation Committee. (This would address the No. 2-, 3-, and 6-ranked restraining forces and the No. 1- and 3-ranked driving forces.)

4. This instructor can become a lead instructor within the department, training colleagues in the use of learning community concepts. (This would address the No. 2-, 4-, 5-, and 6-ranked restraining forces.)

Relations Diagram

The Relations Diagram is usually used with either the Scenario Builder or the Affinity Diagram. It can help a team arrive at root causes and effects of a process or problem. It also allows a team to constantly update and modify the changes in the system under study.

Procedure

1. State the problem

The team should first use one of the other tools, such as the NGP or the Affinity Diagram, to arrive at a consensus on the process or issue under investigation. The team should then analyze the findings with the Relations Diagram.

In this example, the president of a small college was preparing for a $6 million capital fund drive. The theme was "Excellence in the Classroom." The president asked instructors to survey students for projects that would benefit the learning experience at the college. He asked instructors to submit suggestions directly to him.

The college's drama director, Dr. Stone, and the students majoring in drama had been attempting to establish a set design and construction shop for several years without success. They determined that a team was the best way to work through the problem and present a proposal to the president.

After doing an analysis with an Affinity Diagram, the team posted the following header cards to the question, "What are the issues associated with establishing a set design and construction shop?"

1. Get the support of parents.
2. Get the support of local business.
3. Demonstrate a need to the president.
4. Get the support of the student body.
5. Develop and design a plan for the design and construction shop.
6. Prepare informational materials and programs.
7. Help the development office carry out a fund-raising campaign.
8. Organize a volunteer effort to contact alumni of the program.

2. Record the perceptions
    Place the header cards from the Affinity Diagram in a circular
pattern around the issue being examined, as shown below:

Figure 7.20 Starting the Relations Diagram

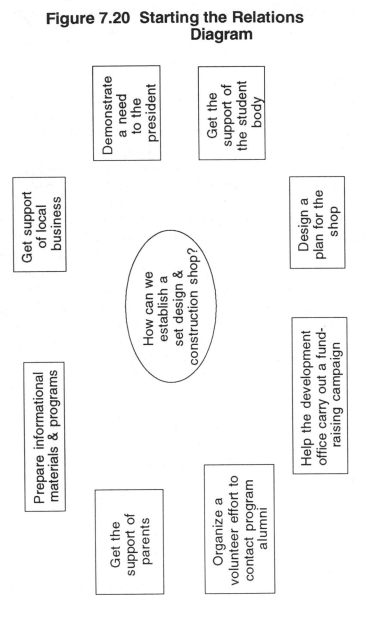

3. Demonstrate interrelationships

The team should determine whether a "cause-and-effect" relationship exists between the headers. If so, draw an arrow to connect them. (The arrow should go from the cause to the effect.):

Figure 7.21 Arrows on the Relations Diagram

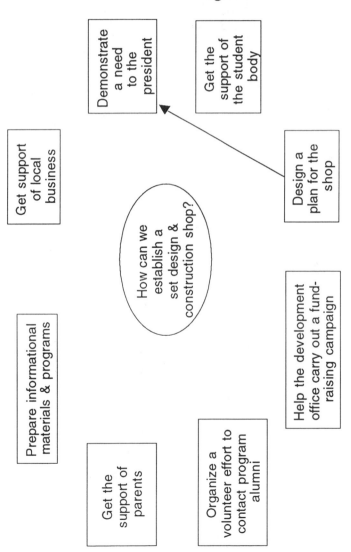

4. Analyze the interrelationships
   Root causes have most arrows going **from** them. **Root effects** have most arrows going **toward** them.

Figure 7.22 Completed Relations Diagram

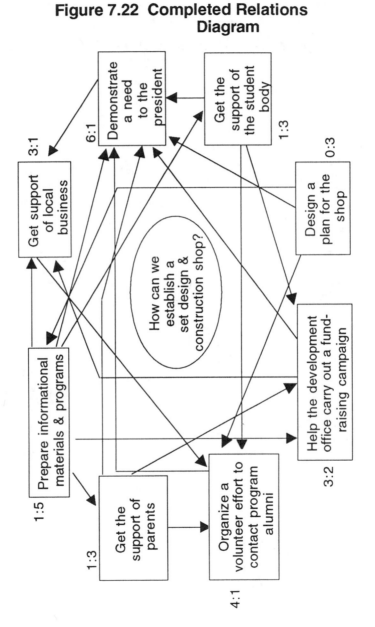

Pareto Diagram

The Pareto Diagram identifies the few significant factors that contribute to a problem and separates them from the insignificant factors. It's a simple bar chart, with the bars being arranged in descending order from left to right. It's best for guiding a team to the problem areas that should be addressed first.

The Pareto Diagram analyzes a variety of effects, such as:

- why students don't do their homework,
- why students drop your class,
- why your colleagues don't take pride in their work, and
- why students aren't learning in your class.

The following example is a case study from an English department. Dr. Salmon's department chair wanted to investigate why there was such a high dropout rate among students enrolled in the first-year English composition course.

The students, working with the chair and the three faculty teaching the course, identified six types of problems:

- poor teaching,
- unfair tests,
- failing the course,
- health problems,
- financial problems, and
- miscellaneous.

Procedure

1. Select the categories to be analyzed

The members of the team categorize the data that they need to collect to address a problem (*e.g.*, time, location, number of errors).

2. Specify the time period in which the data will be collected

The time period will vary according to the system under study. However, the time selection should be constant for all diagrams that are being compared.

In this example, the department chair chose to compare the six categories over an academic year.

3. Record the Data
   Construct a table in order of the frequency of occurrences:

Figure 7.23 Starting the frequency table

Category	Number of Occurrences
Poor teaching	130
Unfair tests	74
Failing the course	46
Health problems	40
Financial problems	38
Miscellaneous	32
Total	360

The completed frequency table shows the category, frequency, relative percentage, cumulative frequency, and cumulative percentage.

Figure 7.24 Completed frequency table

Category	No. of Occur.	Relative %-age	Cumul. Freq.	Cumul. %-age
Poor teaching	130	36.1	130	36.1
Unfair tests	74	20.5	204	56.6
Failing course	46	12.8	250	69.4
Health problems	40	11.1	290	80.5
Financial problems	38	10.6	328	91.1
Misc.	32	8.9	360	99.2
Total	360	100		

4. Draw the graph

Draw the x-axis (horizontal). It should be long enough to display your graph, and it may vary from several inches to six or seven inches. The width of each bar should be equal. In this example, the x-axis was 3.6 inches and the scaling factor was 0.6 inch.

Draw two vertical lines (y-axis) of equal length, as shown below. They should be as long as the x-axis, if not longer, to best display your graph.

Label and scale the axes. In this case study, the x-axis represents the categories being compared. The y-axis on the left represents the number of occurrences, and the right y-axis represents cumulative percentage.

Figure 7.25 Starting the Pareto Diagram

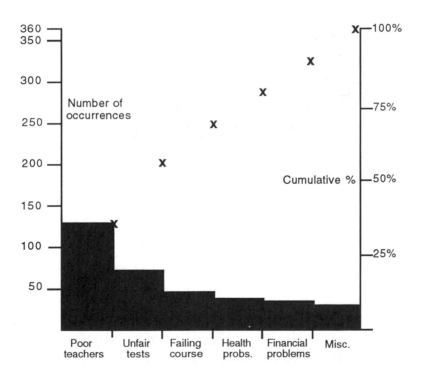

After drawing the graph, plot the cumulative frequencies and draw a line connecting the marks, as shown below:

Figure 7.26 Completed Pareto Diagram

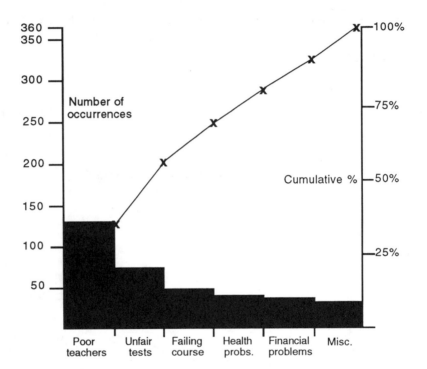

5. Analyze the diagram

It's not unusual for most of a problem to be caused by a few categories, and the Pareto Diagram will easily demonstrate this. In this example, over 55% of the occurrences were due to the first two categories.

Although the Pareto Diagram can point out chunks of data that a team can use to analyze causes, some data cannot be categorized as easily. The above data, for example, could be misinterpreted if the chair simply concentrated on the first two categories.

Now That We Have Our Data, What Next?

After collecting data — including student input, root causes and effects, and possible relationships between factors — the five instructors will analyze the data using TQM tools and techniques.

Dr. Appleton used grades to keep track of her students' success in introductory biology. After the students discussed the possible factors affecting their success, they agreed to determine the relationship between their grades and their study habits using the histogram. Dr. Appleton will also use a Scattergram to examine the relationship between TV viewing and grades.

Dr. Salmon wanted to examine the length of time that students spent to cover material for her English class, and focus on where students were having the most difficulty. She will use a Run Chart to discover the average time it took her students to achieve mastery.

Dr. Wright gave her students homework problems every week. She will try to quantify why students don't complete their homework by using the np-Control Chart.

Dr. Jones used an Affinity Diagram to organize issues and the Nominal Group Process to arrive at a group consensus. He will use the House of Quality and Quality Function Deployment to make sure that the issues are incorporated into his teaching procedures.

After using the Relations Diagram to identify root causes, a team of drama students and Dr. Stone will use the Systematic Diagram to chart steps toward their goal.

Chapter Eight: Building Quality

*"I see no reason to believe that either students or teachers have changed much in this century or that they promise to do so in the next. What **could** change is how teachers, human or machine, go about teaching whatever it is that students want to know or know how to do.*

Within our colleges and universities, such a change could make a considerable difference in what we call an education. It is a consummation devoutly to be wished."

William D. Schaefer
Education Without Compromise (1990)

After identifying a problem and collecting related data, you can most likely solve it by:

- representing and analyzing the data,
- proposing action, and
- assessing the impact of changes, as shown in the Plan-Do Check-Act cycle.

In this chapter, we'll examine how our five instructors used TQM tools in accomplishing these steps.

Professor Appleton, for example, will use the Histogram to quantifiably display the data from her biology class (*e.g.*, student grades, amount of time students spent studying). She will also use a Scatter Diagram to explore a connection between the number of hours spent watching TV and grades students earned.

Professor Salmon will use the Run Chart to plot the amount of time it takes for her English students to achieve mastery.

Professor Wright will use the np-Control Chart to examine when students don't complete their homework.

Professor Jones will use the House of Quality and Quality Function Deployment to help clarify needs and expectations and provide learning projects that will enhance his sociology class.

The drama team and Professor Stone will plot the information from the Affinity Diagram and Relations Diagram into the Systematic Diagram. This will give them a better idea of how to reach their goal.

As with the problems, the tools vary in complexity. We'll begin with the most simple tool and move toward the most complex.

Histogram

The Histogram uses a bar graph to represent how often a class of data occurred. One of its main purposes is to predict improvements in a stable system.

If the system is unstable, the Histogram might take different shapes at different times. Therefore, the Histogram is often used with a Control Chart.

A task force studying a system may gather statistical data about the system and then draw a Histogram to assess the situation. Then, to test a theory, the task force may change one or more processes within the system and, after gathering additional statistical data and redrawing another Histogram, check to see if the modifications have improved the system.

The Histogram analyzes the variation within a system. But to use it, you must have a set of either related attributes (counts) data or variables (measurements) data. Although we will describe how to prepare a Histogram and how the shape of the Histogram may vary, we will not calculate the statistics. Instead, we refer you to any elementary statistics book for the calculations.

In the following example, Dr. Appleton wanted to have her students analyze the relationship between their study habits and their success rate in introductory biology.

The class discussed and agreed on possible factors affecting their success and study habits. Each student agreed to monitor for one month the amount of time he or she spent studying biology. Each student also agreed to keep track of the grades he or she received in biology during the month.

At the end of the month, the team combined all the data. The class members spent a total of 95,250 minutes studying that month. That represented 3,175 minutes per student, or an average of 53 minutes per day for 30 days. The total number of minutes spent studying biology for the same period was 31,399 — an average of 17 minutes per day for each student.

The team recorded the data and made a Frequency Distribution. They used it to discuss ways to improve their grades.

At the end of the first month, the class members agreed to maintain the same studying time, but to study in groups. As before, each student kept track of his or her time. The students wanted to see whether making a small alteration in their study habits would affect their grades.

Procedure

1. Select the data to be analyzed

The team studying a system collects either the attribute data or the variable data. In our example, the students kept track of both study time and grades received.

2. Record the data
   Construct a frequency table like those shown below:

**Figure 8.1 Frequency Distribution of grades
for Dr. Appleton's biology class
before studying as a group**

Grade	Absolute Frequency	Relative Freq. %-age	Relative Cum. %-age
A	1	3.33	3.33
B	3	10	13.33
C	6	20	33.33
D	12	40	73.33
F	8	26.66	100
Total	30	100	

**Figure 8.2 Frequency Distribution of grades
for Dr. Appleton's biology class
after studying as a group**

Grade	Absolute Frequency	Relative Freq. %-age	Relative Cum. %-age
A	6	20	20
B	9	30	50
C	13	43.33	93.33
D	2	6.66	100
F	0		100
Total	30	100	

3. Draw the Histogram
   Draw the x-axis (horizontal) and the y-axis (vertical). They should about the same length and of sufficient size to best display your data. Then draw a bar for each "Grade" with the corresponding "Relative Frequency" at which it occurred.
   The Histograms showing the distribution of grades students in Dr. Appleton's biology class from November 1991 (before group

study) and December 1991 (after group study) are shown on the following pages:

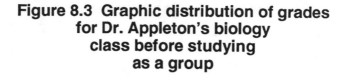

**Figure 8.3 Graphic distribution of grades
for Dr. Appleton's biology
class before studying
as a group**

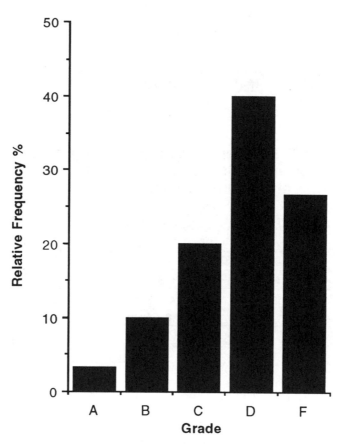

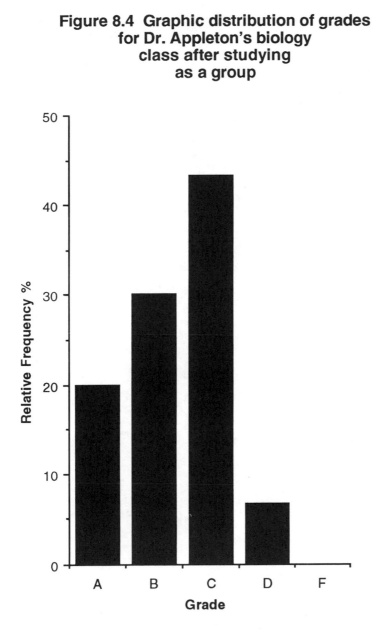

**Figure 8.4 Graphic distribution of grades
for Dr. Appleton's biology
class after studying
as a group**

4. Analyze the shape of the histogram(s).

Histograms have six common shapes, as shown on the next page:

- symmetrical,
- skewed right,
- skewed left,
- uniform,
- random, and
- bimodal.

Figure 8.5 Common Histograms

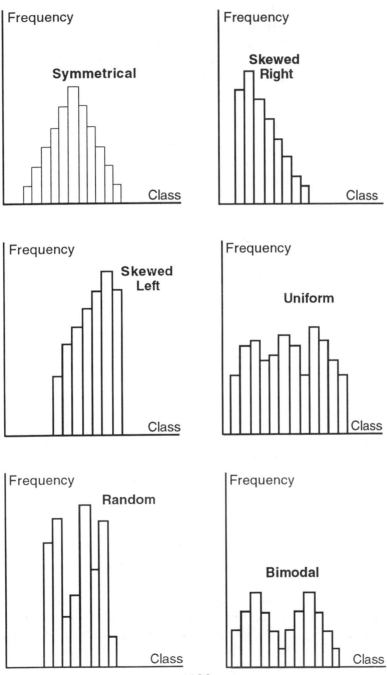

The symmetrical figure, called a bell-shaped curve, usually represents a "normal" distribution, indicating that the system under investigation is probably under control. The ideal mean (average), mode, and median of the class data are equal and 99.73% of total area under the curve is plus or minus three standard deviations.

Histograms can also trail off either to the right or to the left. Skewing to the right is known as a "positive skew," and skewing to the left is known as a negative skew. Both can occur when the data have values greater than zero, as in our example.

The uniform and random distributions can indicate that the system under investigation is out of control. A uniform distribution may also be the result of not having sufficient numbers of classes in your data. The random distribution may result if you have multiple sources of variation in the system under study. In either case, these distributions usually provide little information.

The bimodal shape may indicate that the system under study is the result of several sources of data.

The first Histogram in our example is skewed left. The skewed left, or negatively skewed. It has a larger number of instances occurring with lower grades (C-F) than in the higher grades (A-B). As mentioned above, this skewed distribution occurs when the data within a system have a possible zero point and all the data collected have a value larger than zero.

The second Histogram is also skewed to the left. However, the class grades did improve. In this case, you could say that the majority of students in Appleton's class (93.3%) were able to achieve a grade of "C" or better after changing their study habits.

After analyzing the data, these students decided to embark on a continuous improvement project to see how each could improve his or her performance in all classes. The graphic data was a powerful tool indeed!

Run Chart

A Run Chart, also called a Tier Chart, is a line graph of data where the observed values can either be measurements (variables) or counts (attributes). The data are plotted on the vertical axis, while the time is plotted on the horizontal axis.

A Run Chart is often the initial tool used to gather information about the system under study. Usually, you need more than 25 points to create a valid Run Chart. One of its main benefits is that it examines a system's trends and functions over time.

Various campus departments could make excellent use of Run Charts by posting good and poor trends for all to see and analyze. But you should never use these charts as a threat — or people will refuse to offer suggestions on how the system can be improved.

Depending on the data, the time measured can be seconds, minutes, hours, days, weeks, or years. It also may be possible to add the statistical upper control limits (UCLs) and lower control limits (LCLs) and make the Run Chart a Control Chart.

Procedure

1. Select the data to be analyzed

The team studying a system collects either the attribute (counts) data or the variables (measurements) data.

In this example, Dr. Salmon was interested in discovering the average amount of time it took the students in her six small discussion groups to cover each unit of English literature. She wanted to examine her assignments and teaching styles for each unit, and focus on units in which the students were having the most difficulty.

2. Record the data

Record the data in the order collected.

Figure 8.6 Average time (in days) to achieve mastery per unit

Group	Unit 1	Unit 2	Unit 3	Unit 4	Unit 5	Unit 6
1	13	15	14	16	15	14
2	14	13	14	13	13	14
3	13	14	16	15	15	14
4	19	23	20	18	21	16
5	16	16	17	17	16	14
6	14	16	16	15	15	14

3. Draw the chart

First, scale the chart. This will vary depending upon the type of data you collected (*e.g.*, variables or attributes).

In scaling for the variables data, start by finding the largest and smallest values in the data. In our case, the largest was 23 and the smallest was 13. The difference between the two is 10.

Then divide the difference (10) by 66% of the number of lines on your graph paper. The paper used in our example has 30 lines, therefore, 30 x 0.66= 19.8, or about 20. Therefore, 10 ÷ 20 is 0.5. Rounding to the higher number, each line will have a value of 1.

Next, number the lines from the middle of the chart. Our values range from 13 to 23 days; since the value is one half, the final value is 5 days. Since the center number is 5 days + 13 days or 18 days, we can set the center line at either 15 days or 20 days and assign an incremental value of one day to the other lines.

Scaling for attributes data is similar, except that you assign the first line of the chart a value of zero and add the increment values from the bottom up.

Plot the data points on the graph paper and connect them.

Figure 8.7 Graph paper for the Run Chart

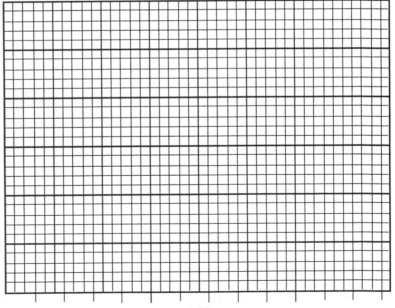

You can use almost any chart paper to plot the data for Run Charts because the process of scaling is always the same.

Carefully label the chart so that all members of the team can clearly understand the results. An example of a completed Run Chart is shown below:

Figure 8.8 Completed Run Chart

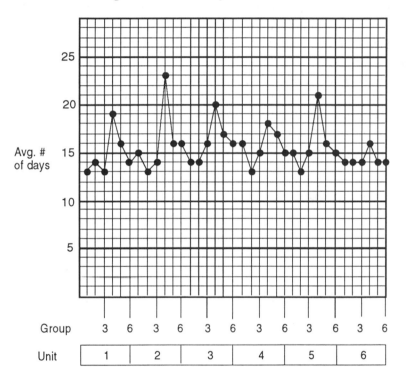

4. Analyze the chart

Look for runs of seven or more points, showing increases or decreases, as well as for other patterns.

In our example, a pattern emerged: students in Group 4 took significantly longer to cover the material than students in all the other classes. Dr. Salmon also discovered that Group 2 averaged only 13.5 days to cover all the units.

Her task now is to match this data with the dynamics of Groups 2 and 4. Dr. Salmon also must engage students in the continuous improvement project, using one or more of the TQM other tools.

Control Charts

Control Charts test the stability of a system. They have a common centerline that represents a process average and lines that display upper and lower control limits, which provide information on variation. Control Charts identify either "common" or "special" causes of variation and prevent over- or under-control of processes.

You draw the charts by gathering samples, called subgroups, from a process, product, or service characteristic. Control limits are based on the variation that occurs within the subgroups. The centerline of the chart is the estimated mean of the sampling distribution. The upper control limit (UCL) is the mean plus three times the estimated standard error. The lower control limit (LCL) is the estimated mean minus three times the estimated standard error.

We'll describe two Control Charts in detail: the np-Chart and the p-Chart. Both charts are attribute (characteristic) charts in that the characteristic under study gives a binary answer (e.g., yes/no, good/bad, pass/fail, or present/absent). We'll also cover two additional charts, the c-Chart and the u-Chart. They are used when the characteristic under study is too complex for a simple answer.

The np-Chart plots the *number* of non-conformances, and the subgroup size is constant. The p-Chart plots the *proportion* of non-conformances, and the subgroup size is either *constant* or *variable*.

np-Chart

You use an np-Chart when the characteristic under study has a definite yes/no answer, subgroups are of equal size, sampling time is consistent, and data is plotted in the order in which it was taken.

Procedure

1. Select the data to be analyzed

The quality improvement team collects the attribute (counts) data. In this example, an np-Chart is used to examine the problem of incomplete homework assignments in Professor Wright's Algebra 102 classes for 10 weeks (30 class days). Wright had 60 students in her classes and she gave a homework problem after every class period. The homework problem was to be returned at the beginning of the following class period.

2. Record the data in the order in which it was collected, as shown in the chart on the next page.

Figure 8.9 Data for np-Chart

Day #	Day	# Students Sample Size	Uncompleted Assgnmnts	Prop.
1	M	60	3	.05
2	W	60	6	.10
3	F	60	14	.23
4	M	60	12	.20
5	W	60	15	.25
6	F	60	2	.03
7	M	60	6	.10
8	W	60	14	.23
9	F	60	17	.28
10	M	60	16	.26
11	W	60	1	.01
12	F	60	8	.13
13	M	60	11	.18
14	W	60	18	.30
15	F	60	20	.33
16	M	60	5	.08
17	W	60	6	.10
18	F	60	25	.41
19	M	60	12	.20
20	W	60	26	.43
21	F	60	6	.10
22	M	60	21	.35
23	W	60	18	.30
24	F	60	17	.28
25	M	60	17	.28
26	W	60	11	.18
27	F	60	26	.43
28	M	60	27	.45
29	W	60	29	.48
30	F	60	33	.55
Totals		1,800	442	.25

3. Do the calculations

The Average, Upper Control Limit (UCL), and Lower Control Limit (LCL) have to be calculated to determine the stability of the "system." Note, however, that a minimum of 25 to 30 subgroups are required to produce valid control limits.

$$
\begin{aligned}
\text{Average} \quad &= \quad \text{total number } (\Sigma np) \div \text{number of subgroups} \\
&= \quad \Sigma np \div 30 \\
&= \quad 3 + 6 + 14 + 12 + \ldots + 33 \div 30 \\
&= \quad 442 \div 30 \\
&= \quad 14.73
\end{aligned}
$$

In this case, Wright totaled the number of assignments not completed over the course of the term (442), then divided it by the number of assignments (30), to arrive at the average of uncompleted assignments per day, 14.73.

The Upper Control Limit (UCL) is calculated using the formula:

$$
\text{UCL} = \text{Average} + 3\sqrt{\text{Average} (1 - \text{Average} \div n)}
$$

$$
\begin{aligned}
&= \quad 14.73 + 3\sqrt{14.73 (1 - 14.73 \div 60)} \\
&= \quad 14.73 + 3\sqrt{14.73 (1 - 0.2455)} \\
&= \quad 14.73 + 3\sqrt{14.73 \times 0.7545} \\
&= \quad 14.73 + 3\sqrt{11.1138} \\
&= \quad 14.73 + 3 (3.333) \\
&= \quad 14.73 + 10.00 \\
\text{UCL} &= \quad 24.73
\end{aligned}
$$

The Lower Control Limit (LCL) is calculated using the formula:

$$\text{LCL} = \text{Average} - 3 \sqrt{\text{Average} (1 - \text{Average} \div n)}$$

$$= \quad 14.73 - 3 \sqrt{14.73 (1 - 14.73 \div 60)}$$

$$= \quad 14.73 - 3 \sqrt{14.73 (0.7545)}$$

$$= \quad 14.73 - 3 \sqrt{11.1138}$$

$$= \quad 14.73 - 3 (3.333)$$

$$= \quad 14.73 - 10.00$$

$$\text{LCL} = \quad 4.73$$

4. Draw the chart

First, scale the chart. Begin by determining the largest number in your data and compare it with the UCL number. In our example, the largest number is 33 and the UCL number is 24.73.

A rule of thumb is to count the lines on your graph paper and multiply it by 0.66. The chart paper for our example is shown on the next page. It has 30 lines, therefore, 30 x 0.66 = 19.8, or ≈ 20.

Figure 8.10 Starting the np-Chart

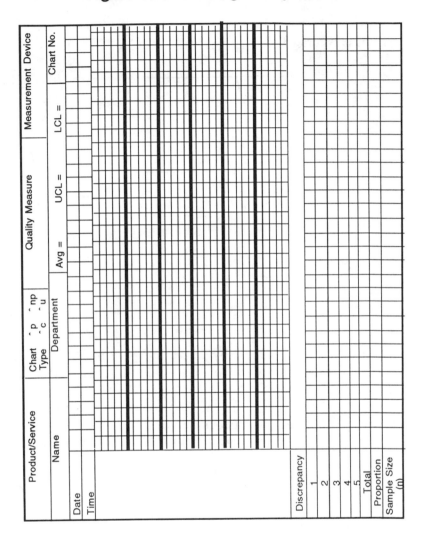

Divide the largest number by 20 to obtain your increment value: in our example, $33 \div 20 = 1.65$. Always rounding the figure upward, every line will represent two in this case.

The lines are usually numbered from the bottom up. The bottom line is zero and every line represents two incomplete homework assignments. (In other cases it may be necessary to label the lines with other multiples, such as 5, 10, 25, etc.)

Wright arrives at the attribute Control Chart below:

Figure 8.11 Attributes for the np-Chart

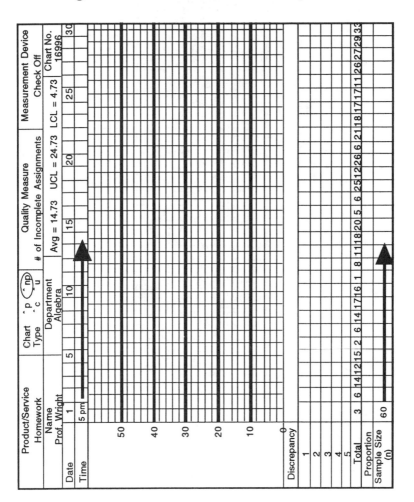

Now draw the center line and the control limits. Then plot the values and connect the points. The completed chart is shown on the next page:

Figure 8.12 Completed chart

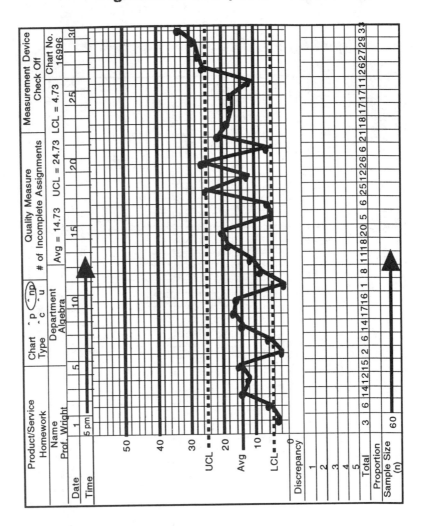

5. Analyze the chart.
   All Control Charts are analyzed using basic rules:

   - Look for points above or below the control limits.
   - Look for a run of seven or more points above or below the average (center line).
   - Look for a run of seven or more points going either up or down.

• Look for cyclical patterns.

In this example, the homework system in Wright's class appears to be unstable. On days 1, 6, and 11, the number of incomplete homework assignments is below the Lower Control Limit line. On days 18, 20, 27, 28, 29, and 30, the number of incomplete homework assignments above the Upper Control Limit line. However, there is neither a run of seven points above or below the center line, nor a run of seven points going either up or down. No cyclical pattern appears.

This system, however, has "special causes" as a defect. Professor Wright could not improve the number of completed homework assignments until these special causes were analyzed and addressed and the system was stabilized.

After Wright examined the circumstances behind the high number of uncompleted homework assignments on days 18, 20, 27, 28, 29, and 30, she discovered that on days 18 and 20 the basketball team had made the NCAA finals; likewise, playing on days 27 - 30, the basketball team was in the tournament. Apparently, many of the students were caught up in the excitement of the tournament, which might explain why they did not complete their homework. Wright's solution: give all of the homework problems after Monday's class and have them returned by the following Monday. It worked!

When first using np-Charts, you may want to assess the stability of a system and then analyze the factors contributing to variations. However, after generating improvements and determining that the system under study is stable, you may want to begin collecting data in a different way. You may also want to stratify your data by day of the week, time, and location, and
then redo the np-Charts. Of course, you'll eventually need to calculate new control limits — but you should wait until enough data is gathered to make the new chart statistically valid.

p-Chart

You can use a p-Chart when you want to plot the *proportion* of non-conformances. The subgroup size may be either *constant* or *variable*. Like the np-Chart, the p-Chart is an attribute Control Chart that studies a characteristic with a binary answer (*e.g.*, either/or, pass/fail, yes/no). For example:

- You may want to plot the proportion of students failing your class over the term.
- You may want to plot the proportion of students not completing homework assignments over the semester.
- You or your dean may want to plot the proportion of graduating seniors who entered with an SAT score below 850.

The p-Chart, like any Control Chart, helps determine "special" and/or "common" cause variations in a system so that you can take proper action for improvement without over- or under-controlling. It helps quality improvement teams determine the stability of a system and monitor a modification.

Procedure

1. Select the data to be analyzed

In this example, Professor Wright's colleague, Professor Breck, wanted to examine the proportion of students who failed his Introduction to Accounting course each term over a seven-and-a-half-year period. Since the number of students who took the course varied over that period, the sample size is variable as well. As a result, the instructor had to use a p-Chart.

2. Record the data, as shown on the next page:

Figure 8.13 Data for p-Chart

k #	Term-Year	n Subgroup Size	np # of Failures	np + n Prop.
1	1-84	100	15	.150
2	2-84	100	6	.060
3	3-84	100	11	.110
4	4-84	100	4	.040
5	1-85	94	9	.096
6	2-85	94	7	.074
7	3-85	94	4	.043
8	4-85	94	8	.085
9	1-86	91	3	.033
10	2-86	91	2	.022
11	3-86	91	1	.011
12	4-86	91	10	.109
13	1-87	91	7	.077
14	2-87	91	25	.275
15	3-87	91	5	.055
16	4-87	79	3	.038
17	1-88	79	8	.101
18	2-88	79	4	.051
19	3-88	79	2	.025
20	4-88	79	5	.063
21	1-89	79	5	.063
22	2-89	72	7	.097
23	3-89	72	9	.125
24	4-89	72	1	.014
25	1-90	72	3	.042
26	2-90	72	12	.167
27	3-90	72	9	.125
28	4-90	72	3	.042
29	1-91	72	6	.083
30	2-91	72	9	.125
Totals		2,535	203	.0801

3. Do the calculations

- Find the Proportion for each subgroup: the total number (np) is divided by the subgroup size (n). In our first entry, 15 (number of failures during the first term of 1984) is divided by 100 (sample size). Carry the calculations out to three places.

- Find the Average Proportion (p) by dividing the total number of failures (203) by the total number in the sample size row (2,535). The Average Proportion = 0.0801

- Record this number in the bottom cell of the Proportion column on the chart.

- The Average Subgroup Size (n) is calculated by dividing the total number of the subgroup size (2,535) by the number of the subgroups taken (30), for an average of 84.5.

- Make sure that none of the subgroup sizes varies by more than ± 25% of the Average Subgroup Size (84.5). You can check this by multiplying 84.5 by 1.25 for the number greater than 25% and 84.5 by 0.75 for the number less than 25%.
(105.6)
(63.4)

Since none of the sample sizes (n) is higher than 105.6 or lower than 63.4, you don't have to do separate calculations for the control limits. If, however, the subgroup sizes were 25% above or below 84.5, you would have to calculate a separate UCL and LCL for *each* by substituting the appropriate number (n) in the formula shown below. You would then plot these points with their separate UCL and LCL on the same graph.

- Do the calculations for the Control Limits.

$$UCL = \overline{p} + 3 \sqrt{\frac{\overline{p(1-\overline{p})}}{n}}$$

$$= 0.0801 + 3\sqrt{0.0801\ (1 - 0.0801) \div 84.5}$$

$$= 0.0801 + 3\sqrt{0.0801\ (0.9199) \div 84.5}$$

$$= 0.0801 + 3\sqrt{0.0737 \div 84.5}$$

$$= 0.0801 + 3\ \ (0.02953)$$

$$UCL = 0.1687$$

$$LCL = \overline{p} - 3 \sqrt{\frac{\overline{p\ (1-\overline{p})}}{n}}$$

$$= 0.0801 - 0.0886$$

$$LCL = 0$$

4. Draw the chart
    You scale and plot the chart in exactly the same manner as for the np-Chart. The largest proportion of failures in this example is 0.275, and 66% of the number of lines in our graph is 20; therefore, each line has to be 0.275 ÷ 20 = 0.014. Since you always adjust upward, each line represents 0.020.

The completed chart is shown below.

Figure 8.14 Completed p-Chart

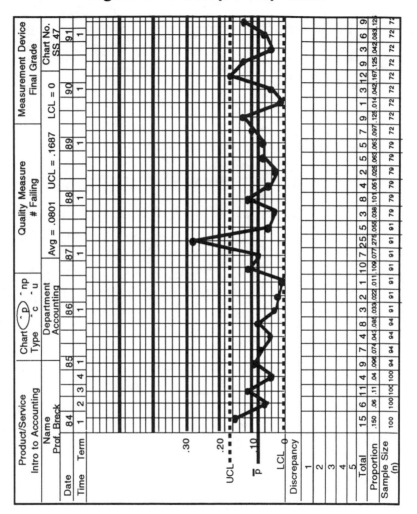

5. Analyze the chart
   All Control Charts are analyzed using basic rules:

   • Look for points above or below the control limits.

- Look for a run of seven or more points above or below the average (center line).
- Look for a run of seven or more points going up or down.
- Look for cyclical patterns.

In this example, the system appears to be unstable, since one of the points lies outside the UCL (the second term of 1987, when the percentage of failures [0.275] is above the Upper Control Limit line [0.1687]). However, there is no run of seven points above or below the center line, nor is there a run of seven points going either up down, nor are there any cyclical patterns.

This system appears to have "special cause" as a defect. The instructor can't implement TQM processes to raise the percentage of passing students until these special causes are analyzed and addressed and the system is stabilized.

After Breck examined what had occurred during that time, he found that the local steel mill had announced massive layoffs, and that it would be phasing out its operations in that area over the next several years. Since the mill employed many students as part-time laborers and their parents as full-time employees, many students were more concerned about having to either relocate or find other employment to pay for their education. A check of the records indicated that an unusually high rate of failing grades permeated the college that particular term.

When this special cause is removed, the system can be considered stable, and Breck may begin to make changes to increase the passing rate. Remember, however, that Breck will have to calculate new control limits when changes are made.

Other Control Charts

There are two other attribute Control Charts that you should know about, both of which can be useful in the academic setting: the c-Chart and the u-Chart. Like the np-Chart and the p-Chart, the c-Chart and the u-Chart test the stability of the system.

The c-Chart and the u-Chart measure the number of non-conforming items. The c-Chart is used when the subgroup size is constant, while the u-Chart is used when the subgroup size is either constant or variable.

Since preparing the c-Chart and the u-Chart is very similar to preparing the np-Chart and the p-Chart described previously, we will present briefly the appropriate use as well as the formulae.

c-Chart

A c-Chart is an attribute Control Chart that is useful when the characteristic under study is too complex for a simple yes/no or positive/negative answer. In other words, the data may have a number of discrepancies per subgroup.

An example might include the type of errors students make while writing a composition in Dr. Herbst's English course. The mistakes fall into four categories: format, grammar, punctuation, and spelling. (If you wanted to calculate the number of mistakes in the composition regardless of type, you would use the np-Chart; if you wanted to calculate the proportion of non-conformances regardless of the type of mistake, you would use the p-Chart.)

Procedure

1. Select the data to be analyzed

Before using any Control Chart, define the non-conforming characteristics to ensure consistency in collection. In this example, Dr. Herbst and her students identified four major problems in the five sections of her English classes: format, grammar, punctuation, and spelling. The students decided to randomly sample two compositions at the end of the five classes for one week.

2. Record the data

Herbst recorded the date, class period, type and number of mistakes, and total number of mistakes in her classes.

The data are shown in the table on the next page:

Figure 8.15 Types of mistakes on compositions

Date	Class Period	Format	Gram-mar	Punctu-ation	Spelling	Total
Jan. 7	1	2	0	1	1	4
	2	2	3	2	1	8
	3	1	1	2	2	6
	4	1	0	1	0	2
	5	0	0	0	0	0
Jan. 8	1	3	1	2	0	6
	2	1	0	0	1	2
	3	3	3	0	2	8
	4	0	0	0	0	0
	5	1	1	1	1	4
Jan. 9	1	2	1	1	0	4
	2	2	1	2	1	6
	3	0	0	0	0	0
	4	1	1	1	1	4
	5	3	2	2	1	8
Jan. 10	1	0	0	0	0	0
	2	3	1	1	1	6
	3	1	1	1	1	4
	4	3	3	2	0	8
	5	0	0	0	2	2
Jan. 11	1	2	1	1	1	6
	2	3	1	1	1	6
	3	2	0	0	0	2
	4	2	1	0	1	4
	5	0	1	1	0	2
	Totals	36	22	21	17	96

3. Do the calculations

- The average number is calculated using the formula:

    c = total number of errors ÷ number of subgroups
    $c = 96 \div 25$
    $c = 3.8$

• Calculate the control limits according to the formulae:

$$\text{UCLc} = \bar{c} + 3\sqrt{\bar{c}}$$
$$= 3.8 + 3\sqrt{3.8}$$
$$= 3.8 + 5.8$$
$$\text{UCLc} = 9.6$$

$$\text{LCLc} = \bar{c} - 3\sqrt{\bar{c}}$$
$$= 3.8 - 3\sqrt{3.8}$$
$$= 3.8 - 5.8$$
$$= -2$$
$$\text{LCLc} \approx 0$$

4. Draw the chart

In this example the largest c number is 8 and the UCLc is 9.6. Herbst multiplies the 9.6 value by 66% of the number of lines on the graph paper. The number of lines is 30 and 66% of 30 is ≈ 20. Each line, in this case, has an incremental value of $9.6 \div 20 = 0.48$. Adjusting upward, we have an incremental value of 0.5.

The completed c-Chart is shown on the next page:

Figure 8.16 Completed c-Chart

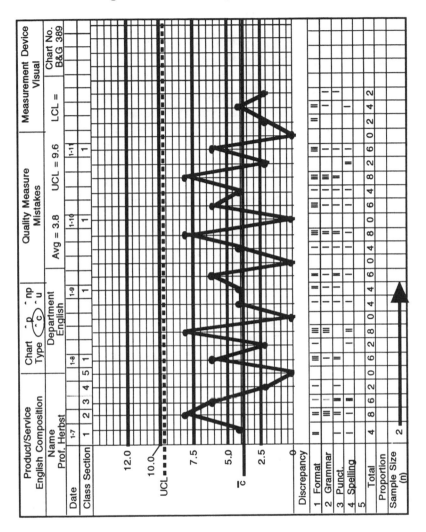

5. Analyze the chart

The above chart does not demonstrate any special cause variation; therefore, the variability in the system appears to be due to common causes that can be reduced by improving the processes within the system.

Both Herbst and the students in all five classes were happy to hear that they did not have to consider any special causes and that they could now begin to work as a team to improve the learning experiences for all.

u-Chart

You can use a u-Chart to measure the stability of a system. Like the c-Chart, it is an attribute Control Chart, useful when the data is too complex for a simple yes/no answer.

An example might include laboratory reports that are incorrectly completed because of errors filling out one of many entries. (To calculate the number of incorrectly completed reports, regardless of which item was incorrectly completed, you would use the np-Chart; to calculate the proportion of non-conformances, regardless of which information was incorrectly completed, you would use the p-Chart.)

But, unlike the c-Chart, the u-Chart is useful with either a constant or variable subgroup size. If the subgroup sizes vary by more than 25%, as demonstrated in the following example, you must calculate individual control limits.

Procedure

1. Select the data to be analyzed

Define the non-conforming characteristics to ensure consistency in the collection process. In this example, we examine the case of a chemistry class in which students were having problems completing lab reports correctly. Redoing the reports was not only a major cause of rework, but for late submissions. A group of students and the instructor, Dr. Brewer, formed a team to examine the root causes of the problem and possible improvements they could make.

The instructor and her students identified five principal discrepancies that resulted in incorrect laboratory reports. (For this study we simply designate them "Type 1" through "Type 5.") They then decided to examine a random number of reports for 25 class sessions. They scored the discrepancies in the same manner as for the c-Chart.

2. Record the data

Record the data as shown in the completed u-Chart.

3. Do the calculations

- Calculate the Average Number per Unit according to the
  formula:

$$\overline{u} = \Sigma c \div \Sigma n$$
$$= 192 \div 103$$
$$= 1.86$$

Place this value in the place marked "Avg."

- Calculate the Average Subgroup Size according to the
  formula:

$$\overline{n} = \Sigma n \div k$$
$$= 103 \div 25$$
$$= 4.12$$

- Calculate the Subgroup Size Limits:

| >25% | = | 4.12 | x | 1.25 | = | 5.15 |
| <25% | = | 4.12 | x | 0.75 | = | 3.09 |

Any proportion number in any subgroup that is less than
3.09 or greater than 5.15 will have to have its UCL and LCL
calculated separately. In this example, refer to subgroups 1,
7, 8, 11, 15, 16, 17, and 20.

- Calculate the Proportions (u) for each subgroup according
  to the formula:

u = number in subgroup (c) ÷ subgroup size (n)

Add these figures to the chart.

- Calculate the Control Limits according to the formulae:

$$\text{UCLu} = \bar{\bar{u}} + 3\sqrt{\bar{\bar{u}} \div \bar{n}}$$

$$= 1.86 + 3\sqrt{1.86 \div 4.12}$$

$$= 1.86 + 3\sqrt{0.4514}$$

$$= 1.86 + 3\,(0.6719)$$

$$= 1.86 + 2.02$$

$$= 3.88$$

$$\text{LCLu} = \bar{\bar{u}} - 3\sqrt{\bar{\bar{u}} \div \bar{n}}$$

$$= 1.86 - 2.02$$

$$= -0.16$$

$$\approx 0$$

- Calculate separately the control limits for the subgroups that vary ± 25%. In this case, you'd include 1, 7, 8, 11, 15, 16, 17, and 20.

For subgroups 1, 7, 15, and 17:

$$\text{UCLu} = 1.86 + 3\sqrt{\bar{u} \div n}$$

$$= 1.86 + 3\sqrt{1.86 \div 3} = 4.22$$

$$\text{LCLu} = 1.86 - 3\sqrt{\bar{u} \div n}$$

$$= 1.86 - 3\sqrt{1.86 \div 3} \approx 0$$

For subgroups 8 and 16:

$$\text{UCLu} = 1.86 + 3\sqrt{\bar{u} \div n}$$

$$= 1.86 + 3\sqrt{1.86 \div 2} = 4.75$$

$$\text{LCLu} = 1.86 - 3\sqrt{\bar{u} \div n}$$

$$= 1.86 - 3\sqrt{1.86 \div 2} \approx 0$$

For subgroups 11 and 20:

$$\text{UCLu} = 1.86 + 3\sqrt{u \div n}$$

$$= 1.86 + 3\sqrt{1.86 \div 7} = 3.41$$

$$\text{LCLu} = 1.86 - 3\sqrt{u \div n}$$

$$= 1.86 - 3\sqrt{1.86 \div 7} = 0.32$$

4. Draw the chart

Do the scaling as described previously. In this case the largest proportion (u) is 8 and the UCLu is 1.86. Take the 8 value and multiply it by 66% of the number of lines on your graph. In our case, the number of lines is 30, and 66% of 30 is $\approx$ 20. So $8 \div 20 = 0.4$ or ≈ 0.5. Adjust upward so that the dark lines have numbers whose multiples are easy to work with (*e.g.*, 1, 2, 5, 10). The completed chart is shown on the next page.

Figure 8.17 Completed u-Chart

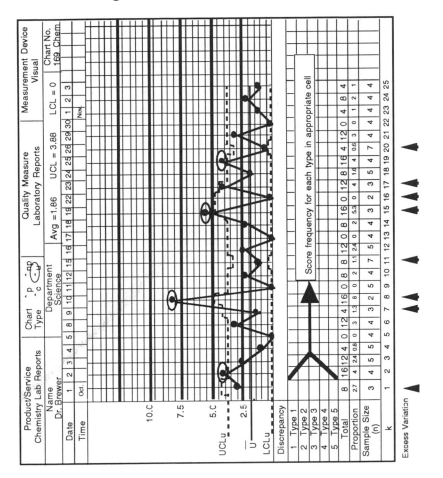

5. Analyze the chart

The chart indicates that the laboratory reporting system is not in control. On Oct. 2, 10, 19, and 25, the number of errors exceeded the UCL, indicating special cause variation. The team can now begin to examine the reasons for variations.

Scatter Diagram

Scatter Diagrams test possible relationships between two factors. If a relationship appears to exist, the factors are said to be correlated. However, you can only verify a cause-and-effect relationship with the use of Control Charts.

Procedure

1. Select the data to be analyzed

In the following case study, Dr. Appleton wanted to test whether the grades of the students in her biology course were related to the time they watched TV. Earlier, Dr. Appleton had learned through the use of the Histogram that her students' study habits impacted their grades. Here, she wants to isolate one specific factor. She asked students to record the amount of TV they watched each week and submit this log to the instructor. At the end of the report period, Dr. Appleton plotted the results.

2. Record the data, as shown in the chart on the next page.

Figure 8.18 Data for Scatter Diagram

Student ID Number	Hours/Week Viewing TV	Math Grade in %
001	<1.0	96
002	2.5	98
003	14.0	60
004	21.0	72
005	21.0	56
006	2.5	88
007	3.0	83
008	7.0	86
009	8.0	71
010	3.0	91
011	3.0	86
012	18.0	60
013	21.0	56
014	<1.0	93
015	10.0	75
016	9.0	76
017	10.0	77
018	2.5	92
019	6.0	70
020	7.5	73
021	2.5	99
022	14.5	60
023	9.0	77
024	8.5	69
025	4.0	80

3. Draw the diagram

Scale the diagram so that both axes are approximately the same length. The axes should be long enough to accommodate the entire range of values. In this example, the time per week the students watched TV ranged from under 2.5 hours to 21 hours.

The x-axis usually contains the data believed to be the influencing or independent factor, while the y-axis contains the dependent or responding factor. In our example, the instructor believed that the more students watched TV, the less they studied and, as a result, the worse their grades. Therefore, TV watching time was the independent factor and the grade was the dependent factor.

The completed diagram is shown on the next page:

169

Figure 8.19 Completed Scatter Diagram

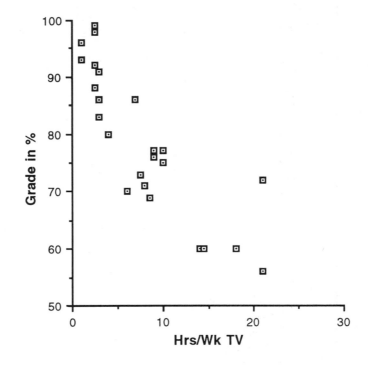

4. Analyze the diagram

Although it looks like the amount of TV watching and grades correlate, there may be other factors, such as the number of absences. Clearly, however, the amount of time the students watch TV might be a possible root cause for poor grades.

Quality Function Deployment and the House of Quality

Quality Function Deployment (QFD) is a flexible but disciplined supporting system for making sure that the customer's wants and needs are heard and incorporated into your teaching procedures.

The QFD and the House of Quality (HOQ) procedure can greatly reduce misunderstandings about course objectives and how they meet students' needs. If used with Personal Work Plan

Agreements (PWPAs), these procedures can also provide a structured way of measuring the performance of each student.

For example, by using the HOQ and the Plan-Do-Check-Act (PDCA) cycle and other TQM tools, quality improvement teams can arrive at a consensus early in the term on how to clarify the presentation of course material.

QFD recognizes that there are several layers in which customer wants and needs are transformed. These layers are often linked by a series of matrices. There will be many occasions when only one or two matrices will provide you with all the information you'll need to accomplish a significant breakthrough in your class. On other occasions, you may have to complete four to six matrices.

We have modified three commonly recognized layers of QFD for use in the classroom:

1. **Effect Planning** translates student and other customer needs into course competencies (see figure on the next page). On many occasions, especially in professional and technical courses, the needs and wants of the students' future **employers** are included, since employers have certain expectations of graduating students.

2. **Effect Design** translates course competencies into instructional techniques.

3. **Process Planning** translates instructional techniques into processes that will eventually improve the teaching/learning system.

Note: a common fourth layer is known as **Process Control Planning.** In it, processes are examined for the best way to control their effectiveness.

Figure 8.20 Example of three layers of the HOQ in which the student and future employers are considered customers.

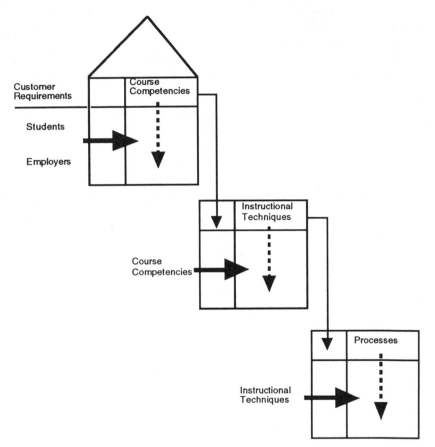

The HOQ is a set of matrices addressing your students' wants and needs and how your course will supply services to meet those needs. The matrices show where relationships exist and may reveal the strength and compatibility of the relationships. A completed HOQ also identifies student needs that are not fully met by your course, permitting you to effectively develop a strategic plan for continuously improving your course.

Let's begin with a brief example on how to build an HOQ. Remember, that the HOQ is a very flexible tool and that you should modify it to suit your requirements.

This example uses the information obtained by Dr. Jones in his sociology class. Dr. Jones' class wanted to do a community service project as a class activity.

Procedure

Step 1: Determine the desired customer requirements

Before you can determine the wants and needs of your customers, you must figure out who your customers are. Customers may be future employers and/or the faculty member teaching the next course in a series. Determining who the customers are depends upon the class (*e.g.*, beginning vs. advanced, general education vs. majors, technical vs. humanities). In this example, we'll consider both the students and the future employers as customers.

It may take the equivalent of several class meetings to determine the wants and needs of your students. You may want to consider scheduling several evening sessions at the beginning of the term to construct the HOQ.

By using various TQM tools such as the Affinity Diagram, Systematic Diagram, Nominal Group Process, and Relations Diagram, you can determine the needs of your customers and reach a consensus with your students about why the terminal competencies, as you have determined them, are important.

Dr. Jones' class used the NGP to explore concerns about student development and an Affinity Diagram to examine a community service project. The team determined that the customers for the project were the students in the class and the community agency they worked with.

Once you have determined the needs of your customers, add them to the standard HOQ form, as shown on the next page:

Figure 8.21 Enter the customer requirements

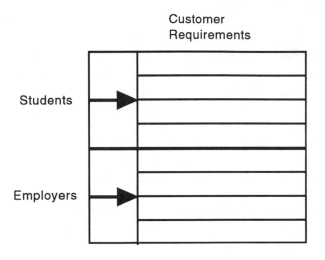

Step 2: Add the performance rating scale of the instructor, as determined by students

It's beneficial to both the students and the instructor if a TQM team of students provides the instructor with the class' consensus on satisfaction levels. The TQM team, selected by the instructor and the students at the beginning of the semester, would make continuous improvement recommendations.

The HOQ tool, therefore, should have a scale reflecting the weekly level of student satisfaction. The ratings should be scaled conveniently (*e.g.*, from 1 to 5 or 1 to 10) with the appropriate value circled (Figure 8.22, next page).

Each student's satisfaction level may vary throughout the semester. A poor initial performance rating for the instructor might be replaced by a high performance rating, just as the faculty member's performance rating of the student may change as the student gradually masters the course. As a result, the performance rating for any student meeting a particular competency may progress through the entire spectrum of 1 to 5.

Dr. Jones' class was quite typical. The student satisfaction level varied from week to week.

Figure 8.22 Enter a student performance rating scale of the instructor

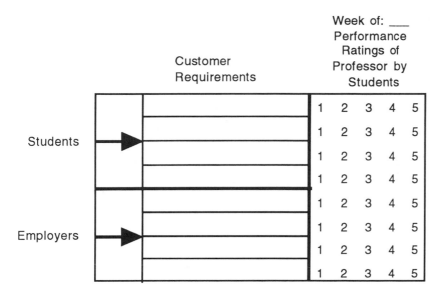

Step 3: Add course competencies and the relationship matrix scale

Determine what course competencies have to be modified to best meet the needs of the students and the employers. Add these course competencies in Figure 8.23 (shown on the next page).

Note the matrix-type table between the customer requirements and the course competencies. We'll describe the relationship as weak (W), strong (S), or very strong (VS). Some instructors assign one point for a "W," three points for a "S," and nine points for a "VS."

Figure 8.23 Add the course competencies and the relationship matrix scales

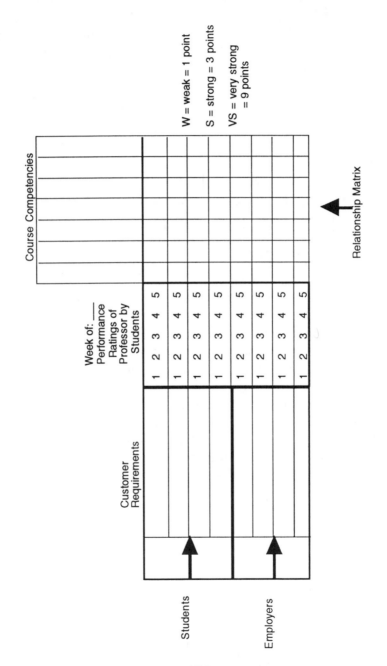

Step 4:   Add the performance rating scale of the students, as
determined by the instructor

The next step is to generate a scale to demonstrate to the class
and each student how they are improving as the course progresses
(see Figure 8.24 on the next page). This requires an honest appraisal
by the instructor and the student. The appraisals should be done
weekly, and should focus on customer requirements, competencies,
and instructional techniques and processes. When necessary, you
should also examine an alternate instructional mode.

Figure 8.24 Add the instructor performance rating scale of the students

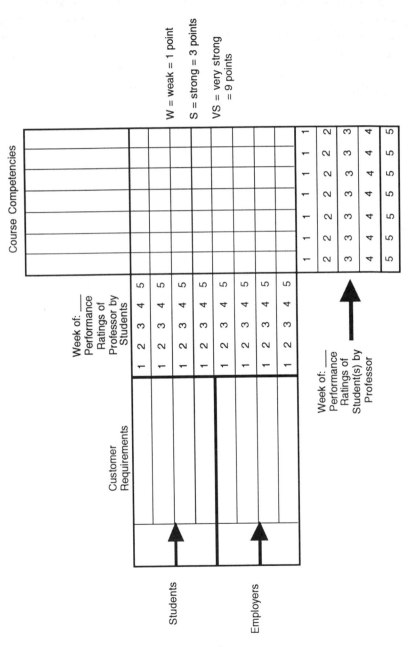

Step 5: Add the roof matrix to determine the relationships among
the performance variables (competencies, instructional
techniques, or processes) of the course

You and your students should examine any relationship among
the performance variables. At the first level, for example, someone
might notice the course competency dealing with "marketing" as
having a "strongly negative" association with the competency
dealing with "business ethics." By entering the strongly negative
symbol ("—") in the appropriate roof cell, you and your students
can easily how the two competencies might support, detract from,
or have no affect on each other (see Figure 8.25 on the next page).

Figure 8.25 Add the roof matrix

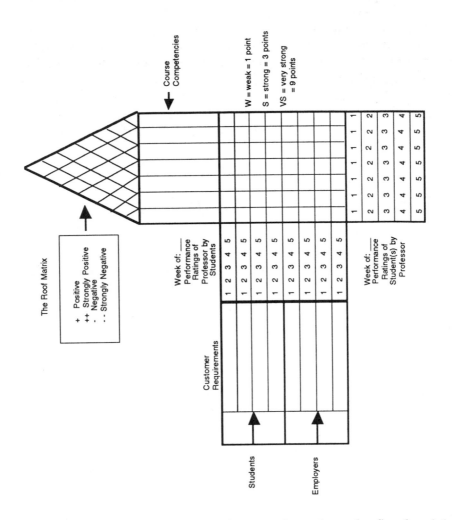

Many courses will not require a roof matrix at the first level, but may require one at the second or third level. For example, when a second layer is added to the HOQ in order to analyze the "course competencies" with the "instructional techniques," a roof might be very appropriate and useful. This is illustrated in the figure on the next page:

Figure 8.26 Roof matrix variation

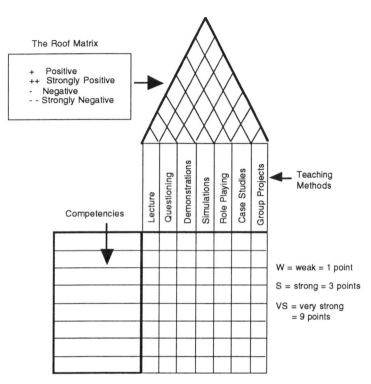

The Roof Matrix

+   Positive
++   Strongly Positive
-     Negative
- -   Strongly Negative

Competencies

Teaching Methods

Lecture
Questioning
Demonstrations
Simulations
Role Playing
Case Studies
Group Projects

W = weak = 1 point

S = strong = 3 points

VS = very strong
     = 9 points

Systematic Diagram

The Systematic Diagram works best with an Affinity Diagram or Relations Diagram to determine the necessary action steps to help you achieve a broader goal — especially if a large number of people, departments, or units are involved.

Procedure

1. State the problem/goal

We'll use the example of a team consisting of drama students and their instructor, Dr. Stone. The group wants to establish a set design and construction shop. They draw the goal on the left side of the paper, using an overhead projector or a large sheet of flip chart paper.

181

Figure 8.27 Starting the Systematic Diagram

```
┌─────────────────────┐
│  Build set design   │
│ and construction    │
│       shop          │
└─────────────────────┘
```

2. Generate levels of events and actions necessary to achieve the ends

Moving from left to right, the tasks become very specific as one level builds upon another. In this case, the team members knew they would ultimately require approval and support from the president, parents, business community, and students.

In order to reach that point, however, the team recognized that it needed to develop a rationale, a design, and informational materials. The team incorporated those steps into the completed Systematic Diagram, as shown on the next page:

Figure 8.28 Completed Systematic Diagram

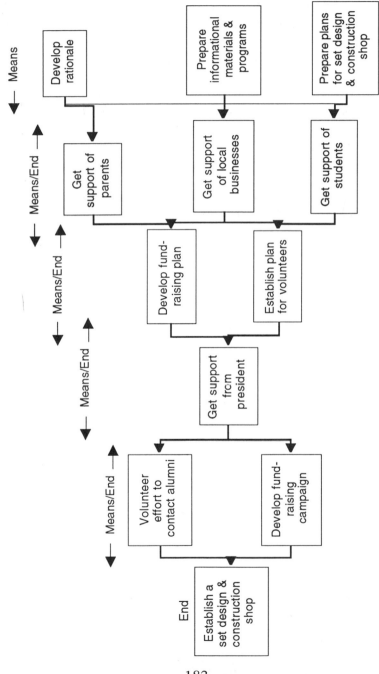

3.   Analyze the diagram and assign tasks

After the team completed the Systematic Diagram, it analyzed its findings and discussed them with the president. Then, it assigned specific tasks or action steps, with time lines, to responsible participants.

Conclusion

Whatever the problem that you're addressing, and whatever changes you make to resolve the problem, your teams need to analyze the results of the changes, to measure your success. Then, the teams must modify their approaches as indicated by their analyses.

As we stated in our Introduction, TQM is a procedure in which everyone strives to *continuously* improve the path leading to success. In other words, TQM never stops.

Chapter Nine: Quality Index Profile for Teaching

*"The quality of education will not be met until
a quality culture is developed.*

*Success can only be achieved when everyone involved in higher
education has the commitment, the motivation, and the means to
embody the culture of quality in every lecture, ... every laboratory
that is supervised, every essay that is written
or paper that is marked."*

William Taylor
Council for the Accreditation of Teacher Education in the U.K.
University Affairs (August-September 1993)

Quality Index Rating Profile

In order to determine the "quality index" (QI) of your classroom processes and systems, complete the table below. Assign points (1-5) for each category subsection, based on described criteria. Then enter your scores in the table at the end of this chapter and calculate your QI.

Self-Assessment Quality Index of Classroom Processes and Systems

Category 1.0: Leadership (9%)

This category examines your commitment to leading your students to achieving quality work.

1.1   Describe what quality means to you. Do you have a formal statement?

Points	Criteria

1   I have no formal statement about quality.

2   I mention quality work only at the beginning of the class, with no formal statement or examples.

3   I give a formal statement to students and share it with employers, business and community leaders, and administrators.

4   I present a formal statement to my students at the beginning of the class. I display quality work for all to use as a model. I make sure students know what quality work means to their own success and the success of the class and institution.

5   My formal statement relates to students and to the expectations of other customers who are committed to continuous improvement of the classroom processes, systems, and outcomes.

1.2   How have you deployed your quality policy and/or mission statement among your students?

Points   Criteria

1   I discuss quality.

2   I display a quality manual in the classroom, with examples of quality work enclosed.

3   I distribute quality manuals and/or policy statements about quality to all the students.

4   I train all students on quality procedures and goals.

5   My students and I work together to improve the classroom activities by discussing the quality policy and establishing a clear direction.

1.3   Describe your leadership in promoting quality.

Points   Criteria

1   I use a traditional leadership role of directing and controlling.

2   My leadership is visible in my concern for quality issues within my institution.

3   My leadership is visible in expressing the quality mission beyond the institution to governing boards, industry representatives, and city and state officials.

4   I am active in supporting adhocracy and collaborative learning in the classroom and implement suggestions that result from student input. I am a supportive leader for **all** students, monitoring progress and constantly seeking ways to improve the learning process.

5   I am recognized outside the institution as a leader for instituting quality.

1.4   Describe your teaching style(s).

Points   Criteria

1   I mostly lecture, with some question-and-answer periods.

2   I make use of lecture, demonstration, and question-and-answer periods.

3   I use more traditional methods, interspersed with group work and research assignments.

4   I use a variety of methods, adapting to the learning styles of my students, including some collaborative learning.

5   I use mostly student-led, collaborative learning techniques with goal-setting as a major focus. We achieve mastery learning of basic facts in various ways. I mix students with different learning styles in order to provide all students with opportunities to contribute in a variety of ways.

1.5   Describe the nature of any ongoing education/training you have had to stay current with the latest trends in your content area.

Points   Criteria
_____

1   I meet the institutional requirements for annual increments each year.

2   I subscribe to at least one professional journal and attend at least one workshop or conference each year.

3   I maintain communication with local and state curriculum specialists, read and implement the latest information, and attend as many conferences as possible.

4   I make recommendations to the librarian for purchases, send for information on the latest trends in my discipline, encourage specialists to visit my classroom to provide demonstrations and/or offer suggestions for improvements, read journals and newspapers to keep current on trends, and make meaningful assignments in concert with world events.

5   I actively engage in national, state, and local organizations and cultivate a network with other professionals. I maintain an ongoing, well-planned continuing education program for myself, professionally and personally, that revolves around a long-term, global perspective.

1.6   How do you define quality in your own work? How do you exemplify that to your colleagues?

Points   Criteria
_____

1   I give no thought to quality.

2   I define quality as traditional evaluation by management.

3   I define quality as student achievement and I present this information in written form to my colleagues.

4   I define quality of work as it is reflected in the students' enthusiasm for learning and achieving quality work. As a super-leader, I am available to assist my colleagues.

5   I define quality of work as it is reflected in the "world-class" quality of students' work and their enthusiasm for helping their classmates achieve success. The numbers of students choosing to pursue a career in my discipline, or enrolling in advanced courses in my discipline are also a measure of the quality of my work. Finally, my students and I are having fun learning.

Category 2.0: Information and Analysis (8%)

This category examines the scope, validity, use, and management of data and information that underlie the total quality system in the classroom.

2.1   **Consider the areas in which you have data to illustrate quality trends in your classroom (materials, student satisfaction, student involvement, employer satisfaction, students entering graduate institutions, students adequately prepared for the next level of instruction in any given curricular area, student retention, time for achieving mastery in any curricular area, etc.).**

Points   Criteria

1   I have no data or just the standard evaluation data.

2   I have standard retention data, with some information on curricular trends.

3   I use statistical methods to monitor processes and systems.

4   I collect quality analysis data and make it available for all (including students) to examine.

5   I use statistical data to analyze all classroom processes and systems. I use the Plan-Do-Check-Act cycle to improve classroom processes and systems.

Category 3.0: Strategic Quality Planning (6%)

This category examines your planning process for encouraging students to do quality work and your short-term and long-term priorities.

3.1   Summarize your principal quality goals, objectives, and plans for the short term (3-6 months) and longer term (1-2 years).

Points   Criteria

1   I set standard goals based on the bell-shaped curve.

2   I set numerical objectives related to quality, cost effectiveness, and customer satisfaction.

3   I practice management by policy deployment, in which all students have work plan assignments related to the quality goals of the classroom mission.

4   My quality goals exceed those of similar classes and everyone is committed to achieving those goals.

5   All objectives of the classroom are anchored on achieving "world-class" capabilities in quality-related performance, which includes process and system orientations.

Category 4.0: Human Resource Development and Management (15%)

This category examines the outcomes of your efforts to develop and use the full potential of all students and to maintain an environment conducive to full participation, continuous improvement, and classroom growth.

4.1   What are your key strategies for increasing the effectiveness, productivity, and participation of *all* students?

Points   Criteria

1   I have no formal strategy.

2   My strategy is dependent on the course content.

3   I have a formal and flexible strategy that encourages my students to participate in assessing the classroom climate and offering suggestions for improving it. Students are empowered to work for the success of all.

4   My classroom environment is completely without fear, and cooperative learning opportunities are essential parts of each class period. Therefore, all students share in the success of the group.

5   I assume the role of a quality instructor, challenging my students to tap their fullest potentials. Students evaluate their own work as well as others' for quality, offering suggestions and encouragement.

4.2   Describe how you educate students in total quality improvement.

Points	Criteria

1   My students receive no education in the principles of TQI.

2   My students are educated only in the TQM techniques that apply to immediate subject matter skills.

3   All of my students are educated in the principles of TQM and TQI.

4   My students are educated in the principles and processes of quality, including the Plan-Do-Check-Act cycle, and use them in their daily work.

5   Learning is based on the continuous improvement of *all* students as the keystone to success.

4.3   What percentage of your current students have ever received education in quality improvement concepts and processes?

Points	Criteria

1   0%

2   Less than 25%

3   25% to 60%

4   61% to 90%

5   More than 90%

4.4 **Describe how you positively reinforce student contributions to quality improvement (e.g., recognition of teams, awards, etc.).**

Points   Criteria

1   I use traditional grades to reward achievement.

2   I use typical performance reviews that focus on individual efforts.

3   I give commendations and other rewards as I deem appropriate.

4   I give commendations and other rewards as my students and I deem appropriate.

5   Team recognition and incentives for efforts are based on improvement of the processes and systems. My role is to support and facilitate the efforts of the team. I post information about team rewards. I have a system for distributing information to parents, community members, and colleagues.

4.5 **What have you done to ensure the quality of environment in the classroom, to make it more supportive, and to empower all students to actively participate in the learning process?**

Points   Criteria

1   My classroom environment reflects an attitude of: be quiet, do your work, and don't question or make suggestions.

2   My students and I discuss and consider suggestions from the administration.

3   My students and I discuss only certain selected students' suggestions.

4   I use a participation management approach, where I encourage all my students to make suggestions, discuss options, and collaborate with others to implement group decisions.

5   I use an inverted pyramid, where my role is to be a leader and to support quality work. All my students are performing that work — adhocracy at its best.

Category 5.0: Management of Process Quality (14%)

This category examines the classroom systems based primarily upon quality improvement processes, including the control of procured curriculum materials, equipment, and services.

5.1   What methods do you use to evaluate your students' academic performance?

Points	Criteria

1   I use traditional paper/pencil evaluation, which I grade.

2   I have students grade each other's quizzes.

3   I grade all tests. Students are able to continue improving their grade until they achieve mastery.

4   Students turn in a portfolio of work at the end of each unit, along with a self-evaluation. I then evaluate the level of achievement for mastery learning at the 80% level.

5   Students work together to evaluate each other's work, including a portfolio of work reflecting cross-curricular, critical thinking, and writing or computational

assignments, and provide appropriate feedback for revision/discussion. My assessment of their work reflects mastery learning at "world-class" levels.

5.2 How do you define "waste" in your classroom and what preventive measures do you take to reduce it?

Points   Criteria

1 I have no formal definition of "waste."

2 I define "waste" as students who do not pass. Passing is determined solely by inspection, such as tests.

3 My definition of "waste" includes measurable external failure costs, such as the cost of dropouts to society.

4 I consider process orientation regarding "waste," such as time, steps, complexity, special projects, etc., to get *all* students to reach minimum standards.

5 I recognize "waste" as a result of poor processes and systems: it includes all aspects of the educational system. As a result, I make an ongoing effort to use curricular teams composed of representatives from kindergarten through college, cooperative learning, cross-curricular teams, and mastery learning.

5.3 How do you help those who supply you with students to improve their quality?

Points   Criteria

1 I make no effort to help them improve.

2   I have an informal agreement to discuss student deficiencies with their former instructors and high school teachers.

3   I provide the students' former instructors and teachers with instruction in TQM and I encourage them to incorporate the principles.

4   Through my efforts, the students' former instructors and K-12 teachers have developed process-oriented quality improvement capabilities.

5   I maintain an active partnership with all suppliers in order to set and improve quality. There is cross-training throughout the college.

5.4   How do you evaluate and integrate the quality of your students' skills that they've acquired in other classes within your institution?

Points   Criteria

1   There is no formal tracking system.

2   I make no effort to meet with other instructors, but I express concern about the skills of the students.

3   I participate in the annual evaluation of skills from cross-curricular classes.

4   There is productive interaction among all instructors across the undergraduate curriculum. We share skills evaluations.

5   Partnerships are formed and assignments are constructed so that skills from across the undergraduate curriculum will build toward higher-quality performance. As suppliers, we are expected to improve continuously.

Category 6.0: Quality and Operational Results (18%)

This category examines quality improvement based upon objective measures derived from analysis of customer requirements and expectations, and from analysis of operations. Also examined are current quality levels in relation to those of competing organizations.

6.1   How do you use graphs to display key improvement data in your students?

Points   Criteria

1   Graphs are not generated.

2   I graph traditional quality indicator information (i.e., the grade).

3   I regularly evaluate traditional information in class, using graphs that students understand.

4   I gather field intelligence data and examine it in graphical form (*i.e.*, the number or percentage of students passing professional certification tests, enrolling in graduate schools, being employed by a Fortune 500 Company, etc.)

5   I regularly use information related to strategic quality objectives and post it in graphical form throughout the classroom for all to see. I provide reports to the governing board, administration, and employers.

6.2   Consider one or two of your continuous improvement projects that have had positive quality and operational results.

Points	Criteria

1   I have no project groups or measurable results available.

2   I form project groups quickly, putting effort into the nature of the project and how it might lead to quality improvement.

3   I use mastery learning and chart the results, but use cooperative learning only occasionally.

4   I establish project groups with assignments that are cross-curricular, global, and meaningful.

5   All my students are engaged in project groups that study issues and result in cross-curricular, global, and meaningful work. I serve as a supportive leader; my students do the main work, using quality methods and tools.

6.3   Describe how you compare your courses with other courses within or outside your discipline (benchmarking).

Points	Criteria

1   I have no comparable data available.

2   I use standard accounting information, such as standardized test scores and students' grades.

3   I collect and analyze data from outside sources, such as employers and former students.

4   I use benchmarking of competitors, comparing percentages of students going on to graduate school.

5   I obtain comparative benchmarking data on all functions and services from the **best** in those areas, whether they are competitors or departments and institutions.

Category 7.0: Customer Focus and Satisfaction (30%)

This category examines your knowledge of your customers, your overall customer service system, your responsiveness, and your ability to meet requirements and expectations.

7.1   How do you determine who your customers are outside the classroom and measure their satisfaction levels?

Points	Criteria

1   I have no formal system to measure customer satisfaction.

2   A complaint follow-up process is in place, but I use the information only infrequently.

3   A formal complaint handling system is in place and provides feedback to me. Complaints are treated as "special cases."

4   I use a Plan-Do-Check-Act process with the information gathered from satisfaction surveys of customers (*i.e.,* alumni, parents, employers, graduate schools). Processes are in place to monitor key indicators of customer satisfaction.

5   I maintain a comprehensive data collection system that leads to quality function deployment for course processes and assignments.

7.2   How do you measure the satisfaction levels of your students and your colleagues?

Points   Criteria

1   I have no formal system.

2   They communicate satisfaction to me mainly through hearsay.

3   I routinely determine satisfaction through surveys.

4   I routinely determine satisfaction through surveys. We also use a Plan-Do-Check-Act process to improve the relationship between students and other instructors within the college.

5   All functions are engaged in quality satisfaction of students and other instructors. Communications are horizontal.

7.3   In what functional areas, processes, or systems have you defined measurable criteria for product and/or service quality?

Points   Criteria

1   None.

2   I measure certain products or services.

3   I measure at least 50% of the products or services.

4   My students and I measure at least 50% of the products or services.

5   I use a total quality system oriented toward data gathering.

7.4   What methods do you use to determine customer satisfaction?

Points	Criteria

1   I don't do any analysis.

2   I track some passively gathered data; that is, I keep a mental count of reports of satisfaction.

3   I regularly track passively gathered data; that is, I maintain records with information and sources on a yearly basis.

4   I actively accumulate and analyze data in areas of customer satisfaction.

5   I am actively involved with all measures of internal and external customer satisfaction and I gather information from employers, parents, graduates, and graduate schools.

7.5   Summarize trends in customer satisfaction and list measurements you have in specific areas.

Points	Criteria

1   I have no information.

2   The information I have is just hearsay, such as "enrollment in this class is up, therefore I must be doing something right."

3   I have specific measurable data available from external sources, such as employers or graduate schools, showing increasing customer satisfaction with the results of the students' work in class.

4   I regularly send questionnaires to other instructors, parents, graduate schools, and employers to identify trends.

5   I collect and monitor data, which highlights key quality criteria showing constant year-to-year improvements.

7.6   What happens in your classroom that significantly promotes continuous improvement to increase customer satisfaction?

Points   Criteria

1   Nothing.

2   I recognize quality successes through awards, certificates, etc.

3   In addition to recognition awards, I send kudos personally to students and parents.

4   I have applied for a classroom quality award and have demonstrated measurable improvement.

5   I have become actively involved in the quality movement not only locally, but also nationally. I have published papers and/or made speeches about the quality processes and systems.

Quality Index Rating Sheet
Transfer your ratings from the previous pages.

1.0   Leadership (9%)
    1.1 _____
    1.2 _____
    1.3 _____
    1.4 _____
    1.5 _____
    1.6 _____
    Total _____
    Total ÷ 6 = _____   x .09 = _____ (rating)

2.0   Information and Analysis (8%)
    2.1 _____   x .08 = _____ (rating)

3.0   Strategic Quality Planning (6%)
    3.1 _____   x .06 = _____ (rating)

4.0   Human Resource Development and Management (15%)
    4.1 _____
    4.2 _____
    4.3 _____
    4.4 _____
    4.5 _____
    Total _____
    Total ÷ 5 = _____   x .15 = _____ (rating)

5.0   Management of Process Quality (14%)
    5.1 _____
    5.2 _____
    5.3 _____
    5.4 _____
    Total _____
    Total ÷ 4 = _____   x .14 = _____ (rating)

6.0   Quality and Operational Results (18%)
  6.1   _____
  6.2   _____
  6.3   _____
  Total   _____
  Total ÷ 3 =   _____   x .18 = _____ (rating)

7.0   Customer Focus and Satisfaction (30 %)
  7.1   _____
  7.2   _____
  7.3   _____
  7.4   _____
  7.5   _____
  7.6   _____
  Total   _____
  Total ÷ 6 =   _____   x .30 = _____ (rating)

Total Quality Index Score = sum of 7 ratings =   _____

We suggest the following interpretation of the scores:

  Score 1.0—2.9   :   Traditional Instructor
  Score 3.0—3.9   :   Progressive Instructor
  Score 4.0—5.0   :   Total Quality Instructor

References

Astin, Alexander. *Achieving Educational Excellence.* San Francisco: Jossey-Bass, 1985.

Bennis, Warren. *Managing the Dream: Leadership in the 21st Century.* Training, May 1990.

Cornesky, Robert A., *et al. Using Deming to Improve Quality in Colleges and Universities.* Madison, WI: Magna Publications, 1990.

Cornesky, Robert, Sam McCool, Larry Byrnes, and Robert Weber. *Implementing Total Quality Management in Higher Education.* Madison, WI: Magna Publications, 1991.

Crosby, Philip B. *The Eternally Successful Organization: The Art of Corporate Wellness.* New York: McGraw-Hill, 1988.

Crosby, Philip B. *Let's Talk Quality: 96 Questions You Always Wanted to Ask Phil Crosby.* New York: McGraw-Hill, 1989.

Crosby, Philip B. *Quality Without Tears: The Art of Hassle-Free Management.* New York: McGraw-Hill, 1984.

Deal, T.E., and A.A. Kennedy. *Corporate Culture.* Reading, MA: Addison-Wesley, 1982.

Deming, W. Edwards. *Out of the Crisis.* Cambridge, MA: Productivity Press; Washington, DC: George Washington University, MIT-CAES, 1982.

Gardner, John W. *On Leadership.* New York: The Free Press, 1990.

GOAL/QPC. *The Memory Jogger: A Pocket Guide of Tools for Continuous Improvement,* Methuen, MA: GOAL/QPC, 1988.

Imai, Masaaki. *Kaizen: The Key to Japan's Competitive Success.* New York: Random House, 1986.

Juran, J.M. *Juran on Planning for Quality.* New York: The Free Press, 1988.

Kotter, John P. "What Leaders Really Do." *Harvard Business Review*, May-June 1990.

Levering, Robert. *A Great Place to Work: What Makes Some Employers So Good, and Most So Bad.* New York: Random House, 1988.

Manz, Charles C., and Henry P. Sims, Jr. *Super-Leadership: Leading Others to Lead Themselves.* New York: Berkley Publishing Group, 1990.

Noe, John R. *Peak Performance Principles for High Achievers.* New York: Berkley Publishing Group, 1986.

Peters, Tom. *Thriving on Chaos: Handbook for a Management Revolution.* New York: Harper & Row, 1988.

Quehl, Gary H. *Higher Education and the Public Interest: A Report to the Campus.* Washington, DC: Council for Advancement and Support of Education, 1988.

Tichy, Noel M., and Mary Anne Devanna. "The Transformational Leader." *Training and Development Journal,* July 1986.

Tribus, Myron. *Deployment Flow Charting.* Los Angeles: Quality and Productivity, 1989.

Tribus, Myron. *TQM in Education,* pre-publication, 1992.

United States Office of Personnel Management. *How to Get Started Implementing Total Quality Management.* Washington, DC: Federal Quality Institute, 1990.

Waterman, Robert H. *Adhocracy: The Power to Change.* Knoxville, TN: Whittle Direct Books, 1990.

OTHER MAGNA PUBLICATIONS FOR HIGHER EDUCATION FACULTY

Charting Your Course: How to Prepare to Teach More Effectively
by Richard Pregent $17.50
This helpful new handbook is written for all instructors who are responsible for preparing new courses. It stresses systematic preparation through analyzing, planning, critical thinking, and evaluating.

First Steps to Excellence in College Teaching
by Glenn Ross Johnson $14.25
This guide helps new teachers to determine course objectives, select textbooks, and increase student involvement.

Classroom Communication: Collected Readings to Make Discussions and Questions More Effective
Edited by Rose Ann Neff and Maryellen Weimer $22.50
These articles effectively address current problems and practices in the classroom – and accommodate even the busiest instructor.

Teaching College: Collected Readings for the New Instructor
Edited by Maryellen Weimer and Rose Ann Neff $21.95
This collection contains ideas, information, and advice on issues confronting new teachers – ideal for teaching assistants and part-time instructors with little or no previous college teaching experience.

147 Practical Tips for Teaching Professors
Compiled and edited by Robert Magnan $12.50
This handbook offers a useful source of tips, techniques, hints, and suggestions for teachers – from teachers.

How Am I Teaching?
by Maryellen Weimer, Joan L. Parrett, and Mary-Margaret Kerns $24.95
The subtitle of this workbook says it all – *Forms and Activities for Acquiring Instructional Input*.

Using Deming to Improve Quality in Colleges and Universities
by Robert A. Cornesky *et al.* $39.95
This book examines the management theories of W. Edwards Deming,
father of the "quality circle." The authors discuss how campus
administrators can implement Deming's theories to improve efficiency,
employee morale, and instruction.

Implementing Total Quality Management in Higher Education
by Robert Cornesky, Samuel McCool, Larry Byrnes,
and Robert Weber $31.95
The authors stress that institutions of higher education should plan more
effectively, especially in regard to resources. This book helps
administrators use total quality management techniques to improve the
quality and character of their colleges and universities.

**Total Quality Improvement Guide for Institutions of Higher
Education**
by Robert Cornesky and Samuel McCool $34.95
This workbook offers a practical, step-by-step approach to solving
problems through total quality management. The authors provides
administrators with tools to increase awareness, build morale, improve
services, and make their campuses more efficient.

**Mentor in a Manual: Climbing the Academic
Ladder to Tenure**
by A. Clay Schoenfeld and Robert Magnan $29.95
All tenure-track faculty should find this book most helpful. It covers
essentials and offers advice from years of experience. A special Appendix
– What Do I Do if I Don't Make Tenure? – may be as valuable to some as
the seven main chapters.

Retirement 901
by A. Clay Schoenfeld $27.95
Thinking of retiring? Don't leave campus without taking this seminar!
Because retirement is more than just dollars and cents, this guide takes you
through each step of the retirement process.

Magna Publications

2718 Dryden Drive
Madison, WI 53704-3086
Phone: 800/433-0499; Fax: 608/246-3597